TEGAN
&
SARA

TEGAN & SARA

modern heartthrobs

MELODY LAU

Invisible Publishing
Halifax & Toronto

Library and Archives Canada Cataloguing in Publication
Title: Tegan and Sara : modern heartthrobs / Melody Lau.
Names: Lau, Melody, author.
Series: Bibliophonic ; 7.
Description: Bibliophonic ; 7
Identifiers: Canadiana (print) 20220254877
          Canadiana (ebook) 20220258279
          ISBN 9781778430046
          (softcover) | ISBN 9781778430053 (HTML)

Subjects: LCSH: Tegan and Sara—History and criticism. | LCSH: Quin, Tegan, 1980- | LCSH: Quin, Sara, 1980- | LCSH: Musicians—Canada—Biography. | LCSH: Lesbian musicians—Biography.

Classification: LCC ML421.T262 L36 2022 | DDC 782.42164092/2—dc23

Bibliophonic series editor: Del Cowie
Cover by Megan Fildes | Typeset in Laurentian & Slate by Megan Fildes
With thanks to type designer Rod McDonald

Invisible Publishing is committed to protecting our natural environment. As part of our efforts, both the cover and interior of this book are printed on acid-free 100% post-consumer recycled fibres.

Printed and bound in Canada.

Invisible Publishing | Halifax & Toronto | www.invisiblepublishing.com

Published with the generous assistance of the Canada Council for the Arts, the Ontario Arts Council, and the Government of Canada.

 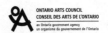

INTRODUCTION

ON FEBRUARY 22, 2015, a good portion of the 37.3 million people who tuned in to the 87th Academy Awards met Tegan and Sara Quin for the first time—at least briefly.

Performing *The Lego Movie*'s earworm anthem "Everything is Awesome," one of the five songs nominated in the best original song category that year (it lost to John Legend and Common's "Glory" from Ava DuVernay's *Selma*), the Canadian twin duo were centre stage for a grand total of thirteen seconds before the floating platform they were standing on spun around to reveal their co-performers: comedy trio the Lonely Island.

From there, the performance became a pretty cacophonic affair: a cast of colourful backup dancers dressed up as characters from *The Lego Movie* crowded the stage, while others rushed into the audience to hand out Oscar trophies made of golden Lego bricks to A-listers like Oprah and Steve Carell. It was a sensory overload meant to bulldoze viewers into joyful submission. As Tegan and Sara continued to sing the tune's main refrain, an emphatic couplet made for children to shout along to repeatedly until the word "awesome" loses all meaning, the sisters weren't entirely lost, but their black-clad petite frames were near drowning in the zippy choreography. At the song's end, they struck a pose, appearing simultaneously gleeful and overwhelmed while flanked between the Lonely Island's Andy Samberg, Jorma Taccone, and Akiva Schaffer.

As a fan of bright, bombastic displays of fun, this moment was an Oscar highlight for me, and has since rightfully cemented its place on lists of best musical moments ever at the Academy Awards. To see two queer artists performing on one of the highest-rated television events of that year was also a big moment for LGBTQ+ representation: "I saw Tegan and Sara in 2002 with 10 other people, total," fan and director Lisa Donato gushed on Twitter at the time, "Now they are playing @ the Oscars?! #LGBT."[1] But as a big Tegan and Sara fan myself, I felt a concerned pang after watching their performance. *I really hope this isn't the thing that they become best known for*, I thought, as I digested a medley of feelings from pride and elation to annoyance and fear.

When you're a fan of an artist, you want them to be recognized for their best work, to have others truly understand what you hear: the melodies that swim inside your head for days; hooks that make you wish you could pick up an instrument and play along; lyrics that induce goosebumps, fist pumps, tears, and more. While "Everything is Awesome" checks some of those boxes for me, it fails in one important department: it doesn't illustrate Tegan and Sara's songwriting skills. The track is a rare release the two sisters didn't pen; the Lonely Island brought them on to sing it for *The Lego Movie* soundtrack. (In some ways, this works in their favour. If you find the song obnoxious? Not their fault! Love it? Their voices are the stars of that track!)

That Oscars moment, statistically speaking, is Tegan and Sara's biggest performance ever. They've shared the stage with Taylor Swift, their collaboration with dance music icon Tiesto, "Feel it in my Bones," has blared over packed festival crowds, and they've been interviewed by TV personalities like Larry King and Stephen Colbert. But the Oscars' reach is unmatched, even as its ratings continue to decline each year. It's a pretty exclusive group of musicians who've had the privilege to perform on that stage.

When I asked Tegan about the Oscars during one of our many calls, all she could recall is the full-body anxiety she felt that evening. "I mostly just blacked out for the experience," she explains. "It was complete and total chaos. Our big thing was like, don't get kicked in the face by the possum doing backflips. It was always a joke with us and the Lonely Island—you don't want your moment in front of a billion people to be getting kicked in the face by a costumed possum." Sara tends to speak in a slightly more severe tone than Tegan. On this, she was even more blunt: "Our whole approach was 'Don't die. Don't lose a finger. Don't embarrass yourself.'"

I shared my disgruntled take on their performance and my concern that most people would only know them from that single, but I was surprised to hear that neither sister minds. More than twenty years since they first started releasing music, Tegan and Sara have learned to put aside external perceptions. What other people think about that performance—and by extension, anything else they do—isn't their problem. Nowadays, the sisters are more focused on how they personally feel and decisions that can help them continue building their career. They've got an I-don't-give-a-fuck mentality that I truly admire and wish to fully embody myself—one day. But as any Tegan and Sara fan who has followed their career since they were acoustic guitar–wielding teenagers can tell you, the journey to this version of Tegan and Sara—the one I got to spend hours speaking with for two years in service of this book—has been long and hard earned.

Early on, it was difficult for Tegan and Sara to not care; the sisters have had a hard time figuring out where they belong. Musically, they've struggled to square their alt-rock and grunge inspirations with the media's interpretation of their songs as folk anthems. They've made sonic pivot after pivot, leaving critics who would try to categorize them constantly befuddled. Were they rock? Were they pop? A part of Canada's early 2000s indie-rock boom? No one knew—or more accurately, no one really tried to figure it out. Most publications seemed content to let other, easier labels take precedence: They're Canadian! They're twins! They're lesbians!

As two young, queer artists entering the music industry at the turn of the millennium, the external perception of who they were as artists and as people reflected back at them like an image in a funhouse mirror. Being Canadian, twins, and lesbians are just some of the many reasons why Tegan and Sara are great and emphasizes why their perspectives are necessary in a culture that's programmed to see and analyze the world primarily through a heteronormative, patriarchal lens. Yet their early years were marred by those same adjectives, which threatened to overshadow the music itself. As musicians who poured their hearts into their songs—penning lyrics that spoke directly to other outsiders looking for a space to call their own—it's easy to understand why Tegan and Sara felt hurt when their art was misinterpreted.

When I spoke to my friend, music journalist Andrea Warner, to discuss our experiences as women working in music journalism—the same industry that has helped shape Tegan and Sara's career for better and often for worse—she managed to illuminate the very reason I fell in love with Tegan and Sara's music the moment I saw the music video for "Walking with a Ghost," their 2004 breakout hit. "My entry point into the otherness of love is for sure rooted in being a fat woman," Warner told me over a Zoom call. "So many different forms of pop culture, and my friends and family, would reiter-ate to me that a really good, exciting, mutually sort of mind-blowing love wasn't possible for fat bodies... And I think a lot of people are told that their bodies, their selves, preclude them from love. I think Tegan and Sara write songs that reflect that, that capture that feeling for so many different people."

While I am neither queer nor fat, I relate intensely to the idea of otherness. It took me a very long time to understand how racism impacted my life, but my mind brims with memories of kids shouting "ching chong" and bullying me for simply being Chinese. When I started dating my first boyfriend in middle school—a popular white guy who was voted Mr. Congeniality by our classmates—his mostly white friends hated me. I wasn't popular. I didn't fit their ideal of a conventionally beautiful girl. I was a girl who hung out with the other Asian girls, grouped into a social tier that was looked down on for being nerdy, weird, and different. I walked the hallways everyday thinking that I didn't deserve his love because people were not-so-subtly conveying that to me through stares and comments. My pain and insecurity later contributed to our breakup.

I may not have known Tegan and Sara were queer right away, but I did pick up on their pain—and therefore their otherness. The songs off 2004's *So Jealous*, the album featuring "Walking with a Ghost" (which I first discovered around the time of that aforementioned breakup), are infused with yearning—for love, for compassion, for understanding. Love isn't guaranteed in Tegan and Sara's music; it's something to fight for. And that fight burns for people who've been denied a certain love, who are told they weren't worthy of the fairy tale ending sold in every book, movie, show or song, because of differences that are out of their control.

At best, reviewers deemed the duo's lyrics "simple" or "oblique," especially cis-het male writers who couldn't find themselves in Tegan and Sara's heart-on-sleeve proclamations because they'd never really been othered. At worst, articles and interviews resorted to blatant homophobia, sexism, and ageism. Tegan and Sara have been asked whether they've ever shared girlfriends and even whether they've had sex with each other.

By the time the sisters finally carved out a space for themselves in the music industry, they were already several albums into their career. The 2010s was an unmistakably prosperous time: they released three albums, including their mainstream pop reinvention *Heartthrob*. Its lead single "Closer" became Tegan and Sara's biggest hit to date, earning single of the year at the Juno Awards and featured spots on shows like *Glee* and *BoJack Horseman*. It was also their first single to chart on the Billboard Hot 100.

After years of not seeing their community fairly represented on music charts, Tegan and Sara had become a pivotal force in queering the mainstream, creating a space that would later be occupied by LGBTQ+ acts like Lil Nas X, Halsey, and King Princess. (And even though Lil Nas X is topping the charts today, a quick glance at the current Billboard Hot 100 still reveals a slim percentage of artists who identify as LGBTQ+.) Aside from making music, they've mentored rising queer artists and in 2016 they launched the Tegan and Sara Foundation, an organization that raises money to help improve the lives of LBGTQ+ women and girls. To cap off the decade, Tegan and Sara published a critically acclaimed debut memoir, *High School*, which earned them a 2020 Alex Award from the Young Adult Library Services Association. The 2010s were perhaps the most seismically influential years of Tegan and Sara's career yet—and the most critically acclaimed.

Despite this, many mainstream, high-profile publications continue to pass on acknowledging Tegan and Sara's talent and achievements. The tenor of their media coverage might have improved over the years—thanks to the gradual diversification of music journalism through the employment of more marginalized writers, such as myself—but the praise still feels fleeting. At the tail end of 2019, I was browsing a lot of "best of the decade" lists in search of Tegan and Sara's names because of the achievements I've already noted. But their names rarely came up.

"I don't even look for myself because I know I'm not there," Sara told me when I told her about my furious skimming of those lists. She isn't as bothered about it as she would have been in the past. Her current reaction reads more in line with the I-don't-give-a-fuck attitude I was extolling earlier, but it's still disheartening to hear her rationalize all the ways in which she knows she deserves a spot alongside her peers—including artists who have personally acknowledged to her how much they've been influenced by the sisters' music. It's clear that the negativity Tegan and Sara have endured during their career—bred equally of both confusion and bias—has forced them to put guards up; they're at times unable to trust the press.

But a determination to keep moving forward, and to do so with a palpable sense of self-love and confidence, is another reason I look up to Tegan and Sara. Their eyes are fervidly set on the future: on the numerous and varied projects they list off with nervous excitement every time we spoke over Zoom; their continued expansion into new mediums; and the path forward they're paving for LGBTQ+ people. Their names may not be celebrated on "best albums of the decade" lists, but Tegan and Sara's influence is nevertheless deeply felt in indie-rock and pop history.

Tegan and Sara are pop's invisible pioneers, queer forces who have fought long and hard to make a space for those who have been othered. The years of work they've put in matter, and I can't let them slip through the cracks. It's time for them to own the spotlight, preferably for more than thirteen seconds and without the threat of getting kicked by a costumed possum. And when music publications—many of which act unofficially as historical records of popular culture—fail to support artists like them, it's time to rewrite history.

PART 1:
THE F WORD

WHO WERE YOU AS A TEENAGER? It's a question that feels easy to answer in retrospect, but in the moment—in the throes of puberty, hormones, and trying out different personalities—pinning that down is an impossible challenge. One day, I was an emo kid wearing all black and drawing fake tattoos all over my arms (today I rock them permanently), while the next I would don a thrifted floral dress with platform sandals, trying to emulate the trends I saw in fashion magazines. High school was hell, but experimenting with my clothes, makeup, and the bands I listened to made me feel limitless—even if in my thirties I now cringe at some of those choices.

But imagine coming of age in public as a musician. The sounds you experiment with, the styles you test out—all of that creates a first impression for the world to judge. And some of that will undoubtedly stick, turning into a label that might not fit, like the "folk" label the media bestowed on Tegan and Sara during their formative years as musicians.

It wasn't uncommon for the Calgary-born duo to casually refer to something they'd done as "folky" in interviews. But it's a word that seeped into their vocabulary through osmosis of what was written about them in their earliest years; it was never an identity they themselves claimed. Yet "folk" used to feel synonymous with Tegan and Sara. Why?

Folk music wasn't really part of Tegan and Sara's up-bringing. The sisters, who were born in 1980, developed a love for '70s rock and '80s pop—the former thanks to their parents and the latter as a result of the decade they were born into. Their household was filled with the sounds of Led Zeppelin, the Pretenders, the Police, and Supertramp. But the artist who would go on to take up the most space, and influence much of Tegan and Sara's songwriting and performance, was Bruce Springsteen—someone who has dabbled in folk-oriented sounds but is mainly associated with classic rock anthems.

Tegan and Sara's parents, Sonia and Stephen, divorced in 1984, when the twins were just four years old. Three years after that, Sonia began dating Bruce MacDougall, whom Tegan and Sara refer to as their stepdad. (Sonia and MacDougall are no longer together, but he remains a strong presence in Tegan and Sara's lives. During one of my interviews with Sara over Zoom in the summer of 2020, he was outside of her home studio helping her build a deck in her backyard.) MacDougall worked at a steel mill. Sara described him in 2009 as "like Bruce Springsteen's people"[2]: the everyday, middle class working man.

MacDougall's collection of live Springsteen albums, as well as VHS tapes of performances, are practically burned into Tegan and Sara's minds and musical DNA. To this day, both can still recall old stories Springsteen told onstage with a reflex akin to the recall of academic teachings that burrow into our grade-school minds, like the periodic table. No doubt Springsteen illustrated the importance of good storytelling both in music and onstage between songs—both of which Tegan and Sara would grow to excel at as their careers evolved.

In addition to the rock playlist they inherited from their parents, Tegan and Sara also soaked up popular music from the '80s and early '90s. New Kids on the Block was their first concert ever. They've always been very open about their love of Madonna and Kate Bush. Some of their most vivid musical memories are tied to Cyndi Lauper; in 2013, Tegan told *Complex* that "My mom had a blue Aerostar minivan and we used to be in it a lot, and we used to listen to 'She's So Unusual' at top level a lot. I can still close my eyes and remember the feeling of the fabric on the front seat and the smoothness of the volume dial of the cassette deck."[3]

All of that music they absorbed would eventually become reference points throughout Tegan and Sara's musical evolution, but by the time they discovered their stepdad's Fender acoustic guitar in a storage closet and began learning to play and write songs, their musical tastes had developed way beyond their parents' albums and pop radio. (They had taken piano lessons for almost a decade, but the piano's rigidity didn't spark their creativity the same way a guitar did.)

By the early '90s, grunge and alternative rock were the new sound of youthful rebellion. Bands like Nirvana, Hole, and the Smashing Pumpkins were revelations to Tegan and Sara, who were in their teens and learning how to carve out their own identities, separating themselves from other people—and each other. Unlike the optimism of the time's mainstream music, grunge and alt rock dug into something darker and messier. Guitars were distorted, melodies were dragged through mud and dripped out like molasses, and lyrics were raw, anxious, and furious. Billie Joe Armstrong sang about panic disorders, Billy Corgan became the voice of a generation of outcasts, and Courtney Love raged against body dysmorphia and exploitation as one of the lone women in the mainstream to enjoy rock-star status.

Tegan recalls taking in Nirvana frontman Kurt Cobain's image through music videos, even though she and Sara were only twelve when the band's breakthrough album, *Nevermind*, came out. Two years after that, when Nirvana's follow-up, *In Utero*, was released, the sisters were in a "full-on love affair with the grunge movement (and style)," as Tegan said in that 2013 *Complex* interview. This crop of chart-topping stars likely spoke to the sisters because of an ability to blur the lines between genders, playing with ideas of what male and female stars should sound and look like; back then, Tegan and Sara were each still in the early stages of discovering their sexual identities as queer women.

As author Sasha Geffen wrote in their book, *Glitter up the Dark: How Pop Music Broke the Binary*: "Love's anger breached acceptable parameters of femininity, while Cobain's sneering caterwaul made him skew more feminine than his grunge contemporaries." Cobain was a self-proclaimed feminist and wore dresses onstage—many people today even debate whether he was trans—while Love's tattered babydoll dresses helped turn a traditionally feminine look on its head and spawned an anti-mainstream aesthetic called kinderwhore. These acts were anarchistic and challenged people's binary views, sparking the minds of those who felt like outsiders and those who were coming into their own sexuality and gender identities. Seeing stars like that on TV signalled to Tegan and Sara that there was space out there for them.

Sara's bedroom walls were crowded with Smashing Pumpkins posters and various magazine and newspaper clippings about them. Tegan's walls were less focused: a Soundgarden poster here, a Stone Temple Pilots poster there, and a large collage of smaller cutouts made up of mostly male celebrities like Johnny Depp, Billy Joe Armstrong, and Jared Leto. A few women graced her walls: Courtney Love, Winona Ryder (on a *Reality Bites* poster), and Claire Danes, who was best known at the time for her role on the teen series *My So-Called Life*. Many of their high-school photos showed the twins sporting oversized hoodies, tees, and baggy jeans along with long, shaggy hair and piercings—a common uniform for teens who embraced subcultures, including grunge and rave, which formed a young Tegan and Sara venn diagram.

The sisters began learning to play the guitar behind one another's backs. When Sara was over at a friend's house, Tegan would sneak into the closet and, using their stepfather's hidden guitar, practice the chords she would see Cobain and Love playing on *MuchMusic*. As she strummed along, melodies began to form in her head almost immediately. It turned out that Sara did the exact same thing when she was alone at home.

When Sara finally shared a song with Tegan—a simply strummed jingle titled "Tegan Didn't Go to School Today"—a collaborative process was born. While the two shared a budding love of music, as teenagers, Tegan and Sara weren't tight-knit siblings. As a twin, it can be tough to assert yourself and establish a sense of individual space and identity; on top of that, Tegan and Sara were both privately dealing with their own burgeoning sexual feelings. Teaming up on songwriting strengthened their bond. Tegan chimed in with suggestions of ways to sing or play, Sara hopped in to sing along in certain parts, and then they hit record.

Music became a glue for the sisters—a remedy for the tension caused by their twin status. Tegan tells me she believes she and Sara are mirror twins, a kind of identical twinning in which the features of one are asymmetrically reflected in the features of the other. When facing each other, they appear as matching reflections, which Tegan says is expressed through the preference they each have for certain sides of their faces: Sara prefers her left side, whereas Tegan tends to like her right. In certain cases of mirror twins, the timing of the fertilized egg's splitting can result in the two siblings being conjoined. While Tegan and Sara are obviously not literally conjoined, it's clear how symbolically conjoined they are from their career choice.

Another bond the two share is their queerness, even though it took them some time to find comfort in that shared experience. Sara was the first to come out in high school and because of that, she felt the brunt of their mother's reaction. Sonia had suspected something was going on between Sara and a friend, but it took Sara some time to admit it was a relationship. Sonia's response, though, wasn't one of disapproval, but of fear and concern for the way Sara might be treated; she was upset too because Sara hadn't been honest at first. By the time any lingering tension had dissipated, Tegan had also come out, and in interviews Tegan admits that she had a much easier time coming out than her sister.

A year after they started sharing the music-making process with one another, Tegan and Sara formed their first band, Plunk. The name comes from a combination of the words "light punk"; it was a reference to their set-up, which lacked a drummer and bass player. Even without, their music was wild and untamed, and they imitated their rock heroes the best they could with what they had. (In reality, Tegan admitted in a 2003 *Canadian Musician Magazine* interview that they were just "fifteen and drunk and screaming through a bad PA."[4]) They performed at house parties for friends and used recording equipment from their radio broadcasting class at school to put together two demo tapes: *Who's in Your Band?* and *Play Day*. Those tapes were sold exclusively to friends and classmates, one of whom told them, "I'm going to tell everyone I knew you guys before you were famous."

While hesitant at first, Tegan and Sara's parents allowed their daughters to pursue music following high school. "We were really unsure of ourselves and we didn't know what path we wanted to take," Tegan said in 2013. "We came from a lower middle-class family, so university was a serious investment and we felt nervous about committing to it, so we asked our parents if we could take a year and play music instead."[5]

It helped that a local battle-of-the-bands competition propelled Tegan and Sara's career in their last year of high school. They were the only high schoolers to enter the contest, called Garage Warz, in 1998—and they won. Their rewards were time in a professional studio, where they put together their first proper demo (as Sara and Tegan), and local fame; they were soon receiving offers to open for musicians like Hayden and Kinnie Starr. In an interview with CBC Calgary just weeks after winning Garage Warz, Sara reflected on the competition and why she thought the judges favoured them: "I think they just see a little sparkle of something that can get to be something bigger."[6]

One of the judges at Garage Warz, journalist Mike Bell, still vividly remembers jaws dropping during their performance. "Just the purity of their voices, the simplicity of the songs, the way they harmonized—they were young, but the pure talent was remarkable." In the days following the competition, Bell called a number of A&R label representatives and warned them to keep an eye out for the sisters. "They won me over that night and they haven't lost me since, at all."

Calgary singer-songwriter Jann Arden, who came to prominence in the '90s, was another early witness to

Tegan and Sara's live performances, catching a set at a local bar called the Ship and Anchor; she candidly told CTV in a 2020 interview that "it wasn't great."[7] But Arden, too, recognized the emotional rawness in Tegan and Sara's music, and admits it was like nothing she'd heard before. Their music was barebones, just a guitar strapped on each body, vacillating between hushed riffs and revved-up strumming, playing around with a slightly limited but effective selection of chords. Each sister penned their own songs, later deciding on the parts the other should sing along to. Their sense of song structure was still in a gooey, half-baked state: choruses were obscured by similar-sounding verses and lacked the bridges necessary to balance out the dynamic.

But Tegan and Sara always knew how to convert little clusters of words into oversized, punchy hooks. Repeated refrains were their key to burrowing songs into listeners' heads. Oftentimes, lyrics spilled out in a cadence that crashed syllables together with a palpable insistence, all carried out with a fervency that that couldn't be ignored. It was magnetic. They definitely had sparkle.

The Garage Warz win quickly catapulted them to a much bigger event later that year when Tegan and Sara were invited to play the 1998 Calgary edition of Sarah McLachlan's all-women festival Lilith Fair. "Being asked to play was like, 'We've made it,'" Tegan said in 2017, when reflecting on the importance of the event, both culturally and for a young act like them at the time. Lilith Fair was created in response to the industry-perpetuated—and patriarchal—idea that you can't put two women on a bill together because no one would pay to see them. "Even then, we were aware of how powerful it was to have so many women on the same bill."[8]

————————

During their gap year, Tegan and Sara worked part-time jobs while finding time to record a few more demos, this time paid for by Universal Canada: *Yellow Tape*, *Red Tape*, and *Orange Tape*. No one ever put a record deal on the table, though, so the sisters borrowed $10,000 from their grandfather to assemble and self-release their 1999 debut album *Under Feet Like Ours*, which they recorded in their mom's living room with producer Jared Kuemper. Originally put out under the moniker Sara and Tegan, it was later re-released with their names swapped, allegedly because they decided the former sounded like the name of a single artist: "Sara Anne Tegan."

The sound of the album was lo-fi and pared down, but that was mostly due to circumstance and limited resources at the time. "Because we toured acoustically the first two years, we were always trying to undo this misconception about us that we were a duo and that we were folk," Tegan told the *Alternative Press* in 2007.[9] Their ambitions, as hinted on *Under Feet Like Ours*, always aimed for something beyond two women playing acoustic guitars. Rock stars, indie darlings, pop heartthrobs—all of those identities exist in the DNA of their earliest works.

When looking back at their teenage selves for their 2019 memoir *High School*, Tegan made an astute observation: that even at a young age, they were already visionaries. (Sara, for the record, over countless interviews promoting *High School*, shied away from that maximal distinction.) While researching the book—which details the messy, emotional years that led up to the start of their musical career—the Quin sisters sifted through countless hours of old VHS footage, photos, and demo tapes. Tegan noted the sheer determination she saw to me: "We just spent hours and hours and hours, day after day, applying so much energy and focus [...] We advanced so quickly because it's all we cared about and I think that's so rad. Men, they're geniuses, but we're visionaries. I think most women are."

Fans are quick to notice that Tegan and Sara have shared mixed emotions—from hatred to pride—over the years regarding their earlier releases, and fear they'll disown work that meant a lot to some of them. In 2019, Tegan and Sara posted on Twitter that *Under Feet Like Ours* is admittedly still tough to go back and listen to, even though "some of it really is bad ass"; I'd argue it shows glimpses of two early visionaries at work. The album, which featured some of the same songs off their early demos, took a lot of risks. It's an experiment with sound and production, a throw-everything-at-the-wall-and-see-what-sticks exercise. Alt-rock elements sit next to piano ballads, orchestral flourishes, and softer guitar moments. There's even an industrial synth track topped with spoken word. "I always find it really endearing and funny that Tegan kind of raps in her early music," Sara jokes.

The album opens with "Divided," an acoustic gem that positions the twins at the centre of their art, long before songs about romantic love took over as their lyrical calling card. "Don't live your life for me or for anyone," Tegan sings to her twin sister, "Live your life as if you're one." Everyone feels the pressure to grow up, find themselves, and establish a career at some point, but on "Divided," Tegan and Sara grapple with what it means to not only diverge from the standard path of pursuing post-secondary education but to do it while tethered to another person—your sibling. The sisters don't sing together much on this track—harmonizing wasn't a strength they'd fully tapped just yet—but when they do, doubling up on key lines as if to underline the significance of certain words, it's clear why they're stronger as a duo.

For author and *Pitchfork* contributing editor Jenn Pelly—I reached out to her for both her expertise in Tegan and Sara's music and because she's a twin herself—this song describes the experience of being a twin in a way she hadn't heard reflected in songs or in pop culture in general. "It's clearly about two people who are preparing to share a dream and envisioning a future together," Pelly explains to me, "and as a twin, I know how complicated that is. Me and my sister grew up with the same dream, and we knew even as teenagers that would be complicated, because as a twin, you're constantly being compared to one another and comparing yourselves to one another. It can be really hard to maintain a sense of self. I think very specific types of self-doubt can come into play."

Many years later, in 2019, when Jenn and her twin Liz interviewed Tegan and Sara, Tegan perfectly articulated just what being a twin—and inadvertently, what "Divided"—is about. It's something Jenn says has stuck with her.

"I believe there is a deep desire in Sara to define herself outside of this duo, like she's cutting off an appendage," Tegan told the Pellys. "It's not sad for me anymore, but it was at first. We are better together. Our songs are more developed together, and we stand out in a crowd together. It's very complicated, to want to sever and tether at the same time, to have this mix of emotions feuding inside you at all times: We desperately want to be apart, and be our own people, but I need her to thrive and survive."[10]

Their singing, whether solo or together, is the focal point of *Under Feet Like Ours*. By turns gruff and saccharine, Tegan and Sara are wildly expressive on each track, as if they're reaching through your headphones and demanding your attention. On "Come On," Sara swerves from a confrontational to an almost mocking tone, as if she's scoffing at her detractors. And when Tegan sings of a job that wastes her time and gifts, you can almost hear her voice struggling to break free of her mundane settings, striving for bigger and better things on "More For Me." Even if a stray bongo drum enters the picture, as it occasionally does, your ears are trained squarely on all the interesting things Tegan and Sara are doing with their voices, like punctuating words at random with a style and personality that sounds simultaneously amateur and mastered. Even as someone who listened to this album retroactively, years after discovering Tegan and Sara in the mid-2000s, I can hear the foundations of their sound slowly crystallizing on these songs.

The same year *Under Feet Like Ours* came out, Tegan and Sara began talks with Vapor Records, a label started in 1995 by Neil Young and his manager, Elliot Roberts. At the time of Vapor's first proposed contract to Tegan and Sara, the sisters were managed by Toronto-based industry veteran Sandy Pandya. When Skinny Tenn took over more of their management responsibilities after Pandya shifted her focus to another musician, Hawksley Workman, the idea of having "an older man try to manage two teenage girls" felt like a bad fit, according to Tegan.

Tegan says the original contract from Vapor was fairly brief, just a handful of paragraphs, and suggested a 20 or 25 percent cut of the twins' profits. Under the guidance of a lawyer, Tegan and Sara declined the offer. Tenn was livid. "He was like, 'You embarrassed me. This is basically a handshake deal, let's just do it,'" Tegan recalls, acting out Tenn's fury. In the midst of negotiations, they fired both Pandya and Tenn. Equipped with only an agent and a lawyer—"We were really worried at that point," Tegan notes—Tegan and Sara continued talking with Vapor for an additional six months before settling on a twenty-two-page contract that the sisters felt satisfied with. "It seems so ridiculous now," Tegan says in hindsight with a laugh, "but we were so proud that we made them give us a real contract."

Vapor wasn't a massive major label signing, but Roberts and Young's pitch hinged on the fact that a label their size could provide a better path. Major labels might not show interest for long if an act isn't immediately successful. Signing with Vapor would allow Tegan and Sara more space to grow and learn—though there'd be less money and more struggles at first. "That's quite literally the best gift you can be given as a young artist is time to develop," Tegan told *Billboard* in 2016. "We really, in a huge way, owe our incredibly long career to Neil Young and Elliot Roberts, because they afforded us that time."[11]

Roberts also supported Tegan and Sara by encouraging them to be open about their sexuality. Both sisters came out in high school, but in recent years Sara has shared more about her struggles with internalized homophobia and her tendency to hide her first queer relationships. Addressing their queerness in public felt like unchartered territory for the sisters, who hadn't grown up with many mainstream examples, especially at a time when the internet wasn't there to help people easily connect with or witness other LGBTQ+ figures. Tegan and Sara often rattle off a short list of visible queer women they saw in music: Edmonton-born k.d. lang, Melissa Etheridge, Ani DiFranco, and the Indigo Girls. Roberts' guidance was simple but reassuring. "We had a conference call with the label, and I remember being really nervous," Sara told NPR radio host Terry Gross in 2019. "I said, 'Is it okay if we do this gay press?' And they were like, 'Of course.' And we were like, 'Is it okay that we're gay? Is it okay if we talk about our sexuality?' And I remember Elliot saying, 'Are you gay?' And we were like, 'Yes.' And he was like, 'Then you can talk about it.'" When Sara asked if talking about it would hurt their career, Elliot responded, "What career? You don't have a career yet. There's nothing to hurt."[12]

Even with Roberts' backing, Tegan and Sara remained fairly quiet about their sexuality in the press for a while. Part of this was to avoid having an auxiliary title overshadow their work, something they knew all too well growing up as twins who drew more attention for that than any individual characteristic. "I used to say it was like Yahtzee," Sara recalls. "It was just like, which thing are they going to be bewildered about now?" For those who did know about their queerness, Tegan says there was, at times, a "grotesque fixation" that definitely amped up their discomfort around the topic. "It felt very circus-y," Tegan explains, noting the details of their lives were sometimes painted as a gimmick. And that's exactly what former *Exclaim!* magazine editor-in-chief James Keast confirms: "before they proved that they had some longevity, musically, the immediate thing was to just dismiss them as a gimmick."

He continued: "There's always a suspicion when young Canadian talent gets mainstream attention really early. Everybody's like, 'Oh, why are they so special? What trick have they pulled off?' In the eyes of the mainstream, the trick Tegan and Sara were pulling off was being lesbian twins." Tegan also notes that the non-musical focus ultimately made them feel less legitimate and less cool, something she has repeated in interviews over the years. "It was just super geeky; no one our age would have read [those articles] and thought that we were cool or interesting. I can understand now, in a much deeper and emotional way, why we rejected talking about being siblings or our sexuality for so many years."

In retrospect, Tegan shows a lot of empathy toward the press because she understands that, in a time without the internet at everyone's fingertips, journalists were left with little to work with. "Like, what were they supposed to talk about?" Tegan muses. "They sat down with us for fifteen minutes, they had [listened to our album] and that's it. There was no story yet, so I don't begrudge anyone, but it's clear that had an effect on us for sure." Sara, also more understanding in hindsight, adds that "no one was really that prepared to have the kind of sophisticated conversation I think we were ready to have" when it came to sexuality. And it's easy to see why this was particularly harmful, even if it wasn't the media's intention; having to constantly explain who you are and not have others truly see you can feel disorienting, shameful, and dehumanizing. Straight people are never asked to justify their existence the way Tegan and Sara have been.

Some might think that having a sibling who also happens to be gay might provide comfort, and Sara admits that having Tegan around was helpful, but it didn't always alleviate the hardship. "It made us extra gay," Sara points out. "You know, it wasn't just like I was a gay person, it was like I was a gay person with a gay sister." She doesn't blame Tegan, of course, but Sara does wonder if things would've been easier had Tegan been straight, because that would mean they both wouldn't have to endure the pressures of outsider scrutiny, or internal pressure to move forward in tandem. "As I found my voice around my sexuality, if Tegan wasn't on the same path as me, well, then that's a new conflict for us," Sara explains.

People constantly compared and contrasted the sisters in other ways, something Tegan acknowledges as a prominent angle in much of their early press. She says she never thought of her and Sara as oppositional, but early interviews and reviews sought out differences between them, which pushed them to identify and exaggerate their differences. But in reality, Tegan and Sara weren't a binary, black-and-white case study. While Sara is now painted as quieter and introverted and Tegan as more outspoken and outgoing, early interviews sometimes reverse those roles.

———

In 2000, Tegan and Sara went on tour opening for their label boss, Neil Young—a rare opportunity for any artist, let alone recent high school graduates. "It was an expedited diploma program," Sara told *Consequence of Sound* in 2019.[13] This Neil Young co-sign boosted their profile even higher in their hometown, as music journalist Jesse Locke recalls: "It was a huge deal. I remember stories about it in the *Calgary Herald*; they were definitely popular hometown heroes."

It was a critical learning experience to see Young and his well-oiled operation, and the kindness he imparted to the sisters was something they took with them on subsequent tours. But, as Sara also notes, the separation anxiety they felt on that tour, away from their friends and girlfriends, coloured her memories with melo-drama and fear—for both what transpired onstage and at home while they were away. "It was such a real feeling of conflicting desires," Sara told *Consequence of Sound*. "I learned really quickly not to be honest with the press about everything, because people would ask us what the tour was like, and we learned to tell people the things they wanted to hear while omitting that I was crying on the payphone to my girlfriend saying, 'I miss you so much that I might die.'"

They were also exposed to a larger audience that wasn't always welcoming. Attendees, mostly older men, would heckle Tegan and Sara, telling them to take their shirts off or yelling clichéd "Freebird!" requests. As with any act trying to get their foot in the door, those first gigs were rough at times. As Sara explained to Terry Gross: "There was trauma involved. I don't want to downplay what it was like to have, like, sixty-year-old men tell us to take our shirts off. We were twenty years old. I mean, it was awful. But on the other hand, it did give us this kind of clever, quick wit that we had to employ onstage." That sense of humour, paired with that innate ability to tell stories they'd picked up from watching those Bruce Springsteen performances and entertaining their grandparents as kids, later became a signature of their live shows—just a quick YouTube search of "Tegan and Sara banter" can lead you down an hours-long rabbit hole of hilarious and endearing moments. "We're funny," Tegan bluntly declares. "It's funny to watch us tell stories." Sara's view of her and Tegan's onstage charm is more pragmatic: "We use it all the time as a mechanism to get people interested in us." Vancouver writer Jennifer Van Evra, who has covered Tegan and Sara's career since their earliest years, describes seeing Tegan and Sara live as "almost like seeing a comedy show; the banter between songs was just as essential as the music. They were really a breath of fresh air, seeing these teenagers that were so talented, so confident, so self-possessed and very funny."

Once the tour wrapped, Tegan and Sara borrowed an additional $20,000 from their grandparents to cover costs for CDs and T-shirts for their own cross-Canada tour in 2001. Being truly coordinated Virgos, the sisters maintained an organized system for everything, from planning travel via Greyhound bus to building binders to keeping track of merch and logistics. Their meticulous nature lent itself well to the band's back-end operations. But Tegan and Sara's business savvy also comes from genuine interest in seeing and controlling every facet of their career. "I love knowing everything about what's going on," Sara explained in a 2017 interview with *Las Vegas Weekly*, in response to a question about her and Tegan's entrepreneurial spirit. "Anything to do with money—and money that I'm going to owe back to people—I think it's just important to understand. I know some people aren't good with their personal finances, but I wouldn't hand my credit card to someone and say, 'I'm never going to look at my credit card statement, go wild.' For me, the business is exactly the same."[14] Shortly after those first few tours, Tegan and Sara promptly paid their grandfather back.

———

Meanwhile, instead of re-releasing their debut, as some artists tend to do when they start taking off, Tegan and Sara decided to fuse old and new tracks together on a new release, 2000's *This Business of Art*. They flew to Toronto and headed into the studio with rising artist/producer (and Sandy Pandya's main client), Hawksley Workman for ten days. The result reimagines a selection of songs from *Under Feet Like Ours* while introducing a handful of new tracks, with more fleshed-out instrumentation and robust production, almost all of which came directly from Workman himself.

Workman's vision for Tegan and Sara was to amp things up. In the sisters' 2003 interview with *Canadian Musician Magazine*, Tegan described Workman's unique, if not dogged, approach. "He said, 'I think people are pigeonholing you in the wrong genre. You're singer/songwriters, but you fuckin' rock out.'"[15] He also thought that they were promising pop artists, something he tried to push for on tracks like the airy early aughts pop-rock bounce of "Frozen" and the bittersweet melancholy of "My Number," both efficiently produced even if they now sound uncharacteristically out of place in the rest of Tegan and Sara's vast discography.

This Business of Art is perhaps Tegan and Sara's weirdest album. It's an outline of the duo's ideas coloured in by another artist, even if he had the right inclinations on the direction they were headed. More often than not, the little details Workman brought in—from the way he layered Tegan and Sara's vocals to the extra basslines, drum parts and string accoutrements—are successful. But when I return to it now, all these years later, it's glaringly obvious that the album is a strange hybrid that never finds complete cohesion. Sara now hesitates to say she was pressured into certain musical directions by Workman (and Kuemper before that), but she definitely feels that she wasn't fully in control at that time and age. "I just felt very impressionable," she elaborates. "When we were working with Hawksley Workman, everything sounded cool because I was like, 'Cool, Hawksley did it, it's great.' But I don't remember, for me anyway, that our fingerprint was really on the music." She adds that she doesn't feel particularly attached to either of their first albums: "I think there's something really accomplished about the kinds of songs that we were writing and the things that we were saying, but creatively, I don't think it really felt connected to our band."

Tegan agrees. "We didn't know anything yet about songwriting or performing or how to use our voices," she admits. "With *Under Feet Like Ours*, we were truly just documenting what we'd written. I feel such fond feelings for that record, but I don't think that we were necessarily influencing the way that it sounded because I don't think we understood how to do that—or that we even could." Of Workman, she says: "He's obviously just a wild, kind of eccentric genius and talent and he was so young and just figuring himself out, too. It was such a whirlwind. We had such little influence over how *This Business of Art* ended up sounding, so that feels like a documentary of that moment of time."

But even as they were learning the ropes of writing and recording, their talent still captured the attention of local and national press. "Tegan and Sara are the real deal," Keast proclaimed in *Exclaim!* back in 2000 when he reviewed *Under Feet Like Ours*. "Their debut album shows an emotional and musical progression quite remarkable for their age."[16] But that review, like many around that time, fixated on contextualizing Tegan and Sara's music within the folk genre, something that the duo continues to vehemently push back against—like in this 2019 tweet: "Listening to *Under Feet Like Ours*. I still reject that we (or it) were 'folk' [...] The production is way more rock than we were given credit for (then and now)."[17]

With such a wide variety of sounds and people influencing *Under Feet Like Ours* and *This Business of Art*, calling their work 'folk' was an oversimplification of what Tegan and Sara were doing. In fact, they were likely aiming closer to the music they listened to at the time: Green Day, the Smashing Pumpkins, Nirvana, and Hole.

But with limited equipment, technology, and personnel, it was hard for the sisters to really create a walloping wall of sound, so their ideas played out more stripped down and minimal. But even then, I still hear their attempts at making something more pop-rock inspired on *Under Feet Like Ours*; for example, "Divided" shares more in common with an acoustic Green Day song than it does with Ani DiFranco. And it's pretty easy now to envision the piano ballad "Clever Meals" instead as a sweeping pop ballad, filling stadiums full of fans waving lit-up cell phones. To me, the album doesn't fit the folk template. When Keast revisits *Under Feet Like Ours* now, he stands by his folk description for certain tracks, particularly "Freedom" and "Proud," though he also notes that overall the album is "a transitional record for them, sound-wise, where they're like, 'This is everything we've written up to this point,' but also, 'This is sort of what we're hearing in our head'—it's sort of both of those things in that record at the same time."

Theirs was a sound that, whether intentional or not, reflected the folk-rock rise in the late '90s. The grunge acts that Tegan and Sara were obsessed with had slowed down, and what filled that space until the genre's resurgence in the early-to-mid 2000s were acts like Liz Phair, Lisa Loeb, and the name that would be persistently attached to Tegan and Sara's career for the first handful of years: Ani DiFranco. DiFranco is an acclaimed American artist whose own music borrows elements from folk, rock, punk, and jazz, but over the years she has earned the nickname "The Little Folksinger." Over and over again, DiFranco's name appeared in Tegan and Sara's reviews, which made them both cringe. As Tegan notes, "She's this brilliant songwriter and she's getting compared to these two turds from Calgary!"

What constitutes folk music is a long-running debate, with some tying the genre back to its roots in passing down cultures and traditions from generation to generation, or its political nature during the Civil Rights Movement. But as time has passed, its meaning has been distorted and watered down, and by the '90s, it was sometimes simply used as a shorthand for acoustic music. Of course, this reductive idea of folk disproportionately boxed in women artists.

But what's wrong with being called folk? In 2012, City University of New York professor Miles Parks Grier wrote that folk, by the mid-'70s, was not only seen as a sound dominated by white musicians, but was also deemed "light, trivial, and feminine," and "was no longer seen as marketable."[18] In a 1989 piece titled "Folk Heroines, Not Heroes" for the *Phoenix New Times*, writer David Koen described the continued dominance of women in the folk genre and how men were getting pushed aside in favour of chart-toppers like Suzanne Vega, Tracy Chapman, and the Indigo Girls. Tom Goodkind of folk group the Washington Squares told Koen in that article, "I think in today's society, a man will pick up a heavy-metal guitar, and a woman will pick up a folk guitar. That leaves Phil Ochs out in the cold. It certainly leaves Heart in a bad position. A woman's place is with an acoustic guitar, and I think it's a sad stereotype that the music industry is pushing. It's gender-bashing."[19]

When subsects of music shift toward more female representation and away from a patriarchal hold, language also begins to devolve into something nastier and invalidating instead of celebratory or embracing of diversification. Andrea Warner has seen this trope come up over the years and succinctly summarizes the mindset of certain writers who leaned into framing musicians within these false folk constructs: "If a woman holds a microphone, she's a pop singer. If a woman holds a guitar, she's a folk singer. And never the two shall meet. That's just the way a lot of people who wrote about music classified women making music." Toronto writer Sarah Liss, who has chronicled Tegan and Sara's career through various reviews and interviews since the beginning, expresses regret for describing Tegan and Sara's music as "folk" in their early days, admitting that "there was an undercurrent of misogyny that informed that aesthetic descriptor, which came with a perceived gentleness—which is weird because the only kind of folk trope that's there on their early recordings was a strummed acoustic guitar. Their delivery, their melodies, and their harmonies are not folk-inflected at all, I would say."

Then there were the DiFranco comparisons. "It's difficult in retrospect to really evaluate the impact that Ani DiFranco had during [the mid-to-late '90s] as a symbolic trailblazer for women, but also as a hugely successful indie artist who was fully in control of her label and her releases" Keast explains to me, a '90s child who for the most part missed this wave of music. "She's one of the last real significant indie successes before Napster came along." But DiFranco's insistence on staying independent left major labels hungry for "the next Ani DiFranco." With an elevated attention toward acoustic music around this time, Keast says that, at least on paper, Tegan and Sara totally fit the mould that so many record executives were hoping to fill.

The folk label also developed a specifically queer bent. In 2002, the *New York Times* declared that "Folk music has become the sound of lesbian culture."[20] But was that the case, or was art created by lesbian musicians being stereotyped as folk? The *Times* piece lists a number of the same examples I've already mentioned, from Melissa Etheridge and k.d. lang to the Indigo Girls and Tret Fure, but painting this batch of artists with such a broad brush erases the distinct differences that made each of them so special. "Sexuality was basically a genre in the 1990s and early 2000s when people didn't know what to do with it," *New York Times* critic Caryn Ganz told me.

Etheridge, whose music is described as everything from roots rock to blues and country (and, of course, folk), came out in 1993. While she told the *Guardian* in 2021 that coming out publicly was "amazing for my career," being one of the US's first out and proud lesbian musicians brought pressure that forced Ethridge to hold back on releasing certain songs. In 2021, she released *One Way Out*, an album of previously unreleased music written before she came out; she'd been worried the songs were too personal, too political, and too overtly sexual. When discussing the track "Wild Wild Wild" on CBC's *Q*, Etheridge admitted, "That's one that I really loved [...] but I went, 'That is way too sensitive, it's obvious that I'm singing about a woman.' And I just took a deep breath and said I couldn't do it, and then I never went back for it [...] It was coming from my fear, and I don't have that anymore."[21]

Tegan and Sara's folk label later expanded to hyphenated descriptors, like indie-folk, folk-rock, and folk-pop. It took several years for Tegan and Sara to shake the folk identification altogether, even though fans like University of Southern California lecturer Chris Belcher felt it never fit in the first place. "I did not experience [Tegan and Sara] as folk because, even though they were playing acoustic guitars, they sounded so different to me than Ani DiFranco," Belcher says. "To me, their sound was very different, and I also think that had to do with their subject matter... I didn't experience Tegan and Sara as expressly feminist or political. They were more so capturing the feelings that come out of pop music around love and heartbreak." After years of listening to Etheridge, Melissa Ferrick, and Dar Williams, Belcher says that Tegan and Sara broke open their idea of what constitutes lesbian music: "I think the folk genre was what I thought of as lesbian music, until I heard Tegan and Sara."

Even as Tegan and Sara themselves pushed back against the folk descriptor, their proximity to the genre drew the attention of fans, too. "Maybe they didn't cultivate it," Warner recalls, "but they were embraced by a queer, activist audience that gravitated toward folk music as the primary agent of their activism." While Tegan and Sara's music wasn't overtly political at first, the twins have been "political from birth," as Tegan told CBC in 2018, thanks to their mother, Sonia, who worked at a sexual assault centre and attended rallies.[22] Tegan can't remember exact conversations she and her family had about anti-racism, equality, or feminism, but her memory—starting at around nine or ten years old—is an amalgam of walking in marches and generally being aware of what her mother did, and more importantly, why she did it. Even then, songs like "Our Trees" from *Under Feet Like Ours* were viewed by some listeners as a glimpse into the sisters' activism and, on that track specifically, perceived environmentalist views. Tegan herself is not a fan of "Our Trees," and bluntly describes it now as "not a good song." And while Tegan's whispery, spoken-word delivery brings a smile to my face whenever I hear it, I tend to agree with her.

———————

When I asked Tegan and Sara if it was true that they were actively trying to disassociate from a "granola lesbian" label, they both fervently responded yes. Sara acknowledges that her knee-jerk reaction may sound mean, but it's less of an attack on the fans themselves and more of an annoyance at the prevalence of certain stereotypes: to identify as a lesbian meant that society imposed certain characteristics or personality traits on them, like being vegetarian or, in the case of this specific label, eating granola. "I don't even eat granola! It just made us feel like we were being discriminated against."

Ganz says it's understandably difficult "when the audience chooses you," but for marginalized groups, identifying and carving out communities around musicians is a meaningful step toward forming safe spaces. This was especially true in the late 1990s and early 2000s, before internet access was widespread. "You can sense that the audience felt comfortable," Ganz continues, "that they wanted to be there so they could make out with their boyfriends or hold their girlfriends' hands. I don't want to take that away from the audience. Even though it wasn't exactly what Tegan and Sara were inviting with the sound of their music, they were inviting it with the idea of who they were."

Tegan, who didn't have a particular audience in mind when she first started making music, echoes Ganz, adding: "I don't want to take away [our fans'] feelings; their feelings are valid. But we weren't granola lesbians. We were ravers and punk rockers. They're welcome to still see themselves reflected in us, if they can, but I'm not in charge of that—they are." It also speaks to a faction of people that sometimes exists within the LGBTQ+ community who promote embracing one's unique identity—while also wanting their public figures to fit into a specific box.

But Tegan and Sara never neatly fit into one box. Tegan is right: they were visionaries—even if many listeners and critics at the time didn't know how to describe what they were doing.

PART 2:
I GET SO JEALOUS

CONTROL IS A KEY COMPONENT of Tegan and Sara's current career. Everything they do, from who they work with in the studio and who opens for them on tours, to media opportunities (including speaking to me for this book), is carefully considered by both sisters. But back in 2002, their main focus was on controlling the way their music sounded. It's apparent they didn't feel like they were in the driver's seat for *Under Feet Like Ours* and *This Business of Art*, but in the electrifying opening moments of their third album, *If It Was You*, Tegan and Sara make it abundantly clear who is in charge.

That thunderous first track, "Time Running," is an immediate reintroduction, a blaring contrast to the mostly acoustic efforts that marked their previous albums, and a proclamation that Tegan and Sara had finally landed on a sound they could call their own. Even though the song is about moving on from a romantic relationship, the urgency in Tegan and Sara's voices also reads like a warning shot to anyone who'd thought to pigeonhole the duo. With the amps turned up and their songwriting sharpened, Tegan and Sara's vision was primed for a wider audience.

Tegan and Sara's newfound empowerment partially came from their ability to write and create more fully formed demos using the music software Pro Tools.

"We created a soundscape for what we wanted," Tegan recalls. This also helped them develop separately as songwriters. They each used Pro Tools to lay down their distinct ideas, which, as Tegan notes, "really made us feel re-interested in the band. Because all of a sudden I could listen to songs I hadn't heard Sara play. I would burn copies and bring them home to listen to, and I really became a fan of Sara's music." They showed these Pro Tools blueprints to John Collins and Dave Carswell, two BC-based producers Tegan and Sara teamed up with shortly after relocating from Calgary to Vancouver to be closer to a bigger music scene. "It was literally our first time being able to say, 'Here's all the demos,' and 'Here's, like, the half-time beat I want to use and the weird shaker sound I want,'" Tegan added.

The sound on *If It Was You* was closely modelled after the indie-rock scene that was bubbling up, especially in Canada, with bands like the New Pornographers (Collins was a producer and Carswell a member), Broken Social Scene, Hot Hot Heat, and the Constantines. A genre born in the '80s and '90s thanks to groups like the Smiths and R.E.M., indie-rock was oftentimes used interchangeably with alt-rock; it came to refer to acts that operated independently outside of the major label system and maintained a connection with underground subcultures. For Tegan and Sara, Canada's burgeoning indie scene felt like the perfect fit. They were excited at the idea of finally fitting in somewhere, according to Sara: "We found indie-rock and it was a style that worked for us."

But *If It Was You* also conveyed a pop ambition that feels even more evident in retrospect. "They weren't going to bend over backward or anything like that, but they wanted to be successful," Collins remembers. In the early 2000s, the idea of poptimism—a belief that pop music was worthy of critique, as opposed to being valueless—was only beginning to germinate. Strict borders dividing pop from rock from hip hop and so on were still enforced, and many journalists still held rock music up as the true art form because it was built on authenticity. Tegan and Sara's blend of rock and pop wasn't uncommon, and their indie-rock peers found themselves on the receiving end of rockist praise. Tegan and Sara, on the other hand, were repositioned by some in the press as rising pop artists alongside Avril Lavigne and Michelle Branch, perhaps because of their age, their gender, that pop ambition, or some strange cocktail of all three.

As two alt-rock and pop-punk lovers, entering the 2000s felt alien to Tegan and Sara. The grunge scene the sisters saw top the charts in the 1990s ceded to re-cord-breaking pop acts like Britney Spears, Backstreet Boys, and *NSYNC, and suddenly, a space Tegan and Sara thought they could inhabit morphed into some-thing that felt decidedly less welcoming to outsiders. While Sara still maintains she was anti-pop then, Tegan openly admits that they consumed pop music. But the idea of possibly ascending into a mainstream that was dominated by—and mainly serving and benefitting—the male gaze concerned Tegan. Their initial rejection of pop stars, Tegan clarifies now, was just "a preemptive strike against what we feared would happen to us as women in the industry."

The weight women bear in music can feel crushing, especially when it's compounded by the intersections of sexuality, race, class, and more. As two gay siblings just entering their twenties who didn't conform to a traditionally feminine image—Tegan and Sara's signature look at the time included short, spiky hair, no makeup, and clothes that weren't revealing or form-fitting—being judged for their appearance and by extension their identity as queer twins was a part of their jobs that they honestly hadn't prepared for. Without seeing examples of other young queer women charting their own course, how could they? "I don't think we necessarily had the adult language yet," Sara says now of the music industry and media's emphasis on sexuality and objectification, "to say like, that's inappropriate, and it's not Britney's fault, but a larger systemic problem."

Sara's insistence on distancing themselves from the world of pop, which is constantly plagued by criticisms of artificiality, was fuelled by the sting from early press insinuating that Tegan and Sara were a gimmick. "We were constantly battling that pressure from both sides," Sara says now. "It was like, 'Do not act like Britney Spears and the pop machine that everyone thinks spit you two out,' but also, 'Oh my God, you're so off-putting, like, someone shove a sock in their mouths.' We were opinionated, we sang in a masculine way, we throttled our guitars, and I think that really bothered people and turned them off of what we did. Like, what the fuck were we supposed to do?"

If It Was You crystallized Tegan and Sara's already solid hooks into iron-clad earworms that I still return to today; it holds up as some of their strongest work. Most songs on this album are three-and-a-half minutes or less, and choruses eat up much of each track's runtime, but not in a bad way. Romantic love continues to rule their lyrics, but there's a maturity to the way Tegan and Sara write and sing about it on this album. Tegan captures that early twenties feeling—when relationships grow more complicated and one's understanding of love can feel increasingly less transparent—on "You Went Away": "Is there more to life than love and being together?"

On that track's second verse, she sings, "You went away/ because you said you couldn't love me/ And I went away/ because all I do is love you," an explicit line that may cut even deeper for queer fans. In 2005, a fan on LiveJournal reflected on the radical omission of gendered pronouns, writing,

'He' and 'she' pronouns are replaced with 'you' and 'we' and 'they' so that any listener can relate. Straight girls can feel like the songs are written for them, guys can feel like the songs are written about them, and lesbians can smile in the knowledge that someone is putting out solid pop songs from their perspective.[23]

"Living Room," a fan favourite to this day, blends their acoustic past with the plugged-in vigour of their more rock-leaning sound. Mixing banjo, guitar, and a hearty drum beat—in addition to a kitchen sink's worth of flourishes added in by Collins and Carswell—Tegan gives one of her most thrilling vocal performances, stretching her range up to a falsetto howl then down to a guttural rasp that distinguishes her vocals from Sara's, who perfectly complements Tegan on harmony.

Tegan has said in the past that "Living Room" isn't explicitly personal. In the most literal sense, she found the inspiration for this track while living alone in an apartment where her living room window looked directly into another unit across from her. In her six months there, she only ever peered into the other apartment twice, because the tenants kept their blinds closed almost the entire time. On one of those occasions, she'd stumbled into her living room in the middle of the night, groggy from cold medication. Noticing that her apartment was suddenly lit up, she looked across.

"There was this man standing there, like this huge guy, fat guy, hairy, no shirt on," she described in a 2003 interview with pomn.com. "And he's staring into my apartment and it was dark and there was this frail little young woman, probably in her mid-thirties, bawling hysterically and they're both just standing there [...] I thought it was really sad that she was crying. Like, it was such a weird, odd moment. So, I tried to sort of act as if I knew her or something when I wrote it."[24]

In that interview, Tegan concludes that the song is "like a joke," but fans sensed that wasn't the whole story. In the minds of listeners, the relationship between her and the subject is romantic—either Tegan had dated her or was in love with her. (While I had always been vaguely aware of the romantic undertones of this song, I admittedly never tried to untangle its exact meaning until researching this book.) A fan online theorized that "when she's looking through the windows, into the person's house, she's looking back on the relationship."[25] The impassioned delivery of the chorus, where she sings of losing her mind, feels too intimate. For a song that Tegan once shrugged off as impersonal, certain fans believe it to be the complete opposite. It's yet another moment where they see Tegan and Sara's music speaking a secret, coded language just for them.

"I am quite glad it's a queer anthem," Tegan tells me, affirming that the truth lies somewhere between the story she once told—which was real, she contends—and a reflection on a complicated, on-again-off-again relationship with a woman who was her total opposite. "Her bathroom was messy, and I was—and still am—a clean freak," Tegan explains. On "Living Room," that dichotomy is right there in the second verse:

My windows look into your bathroom
Well I spend the evening watching you get yourself clean
And I wonder why it is that they left this bathroom
So unclean, so unlike me

"When I wrote the song, we were in a phase where we weren't really communicating," Tegan continues. "When I would hear from her, it was at odd times of the day. She would go missing for days at a time, and I often found myself walking past her building and trying to see if she was home, just to see if she was okay. But her building was incredibly tall. She lived on the 18th floor and I would stand outside counting the windows, trying to see if I could see her lights on. She was recovering from a bad relationship and I think I was feeling quite emo and tortured over her ghosting me, while also being very empathetic about her situation and her broken heart."

Much of that nuance felt lost in the press' writing around this record. Some argued Tegan and Sara's songwriting wasn't sophisticated enough. Others praised their new sound, but skipped over the heart-wrenching truths beneath the hooks. And in spite of positive reviews—and to be clear, most of them were positive—critics leaned too much on genre-based descriptors. Any acclaim was overwhelmed by other references points, like Tegan and Sara's "Ani DiFranco-ish"[26] past or describing *If It Was You* as "acousta-grrrl folk"[27] or "alt-punk"[28] or belonging in the needlessly narrow "young female singer/songwriter subgenre."[29]

The urge for reviewers to give a framework for readers to understand the music they're writing about is longstanding. Every journalist alive, myself included, has compared an artist to someone else as a form of shorthand. But the over-reliance on this practice feels like a crutch for something bigger, especially in regards to Tegan and Sara's music. When reading back on various reviews, I often felt like writers plugged in bands or genres to cover up a lack of understanding or knowledge of how to truly write about an act with as many levels of complexity as Tegan and Sara. A lot of the time, that correlated to cis-het white men who had the privilege of owning those bylines.

———

Tegan and Sara forged on with their next album, 2004's *So Jealous*. By that point, indie-rock had solidified into a distinct genre that was bubbling up to the surface of mainstream primetime TV shows like *Grey's Anatomy* and *The O.C.*, which acted as launching pads for acts like Death Cab For Cutie, Snow Patrol, and Modest Mouse.

There's a good argument to be made for 2004 as the exact year that solidified Canada's place on the indie-rock map. While bands like the New Pornographers, Broken Social Scene, and Metric started percolating across the country at the tail end of the '90s, Canada maintained an inferiority complex for years that was hard to shake. "Canadian artists were almost like second class," Jennifer Van Evra explains. "There wasn't the pride in Canadian music that we have now." Even with the Canadian Radio-television and Telecommunications Commission (CRTC) enforcing Canadian content rules that required stations to play a sizable percentage of homegrown acts, it was challenging for independent artists to elbow their way into a regular rotation that mostly stayed loyal to major label stars like Avril Lavigne, Simple Plan, and Nelly Furtado.

This is where the internet comes in. While it took a few years for Google to rise to ubiquity, by 2004, the popular online search engine attracted 200 million searches a day. In the US alone, more than 60 percent of households owned a computer. In my household, we had two computers: one permanently off-limits in my older brother's room and another slightly more accessible one in my older sister's room. It was on my sister's computer that I first began obsessively following blogs like *Pitchfork*, *Chromewaves*, and *Fluxblog*, in search of new music outside the mainstream sphere.

Online music blogs were emerging as authorities, chipping away at the power that physical magazines and newspapers had long held. MP3-oriented sites served as a sampling platter for wide-eyed fans looking to preview someone's work before downloading or buying a full album. Best yet, they kickstarted the disintegration of geographical borders. Suddenly, discovering a singer from Sweden or Japan didn't require hopping on a plane. And for Canadians, that meant a levelling of the playing field, especially with a larger, more intimidating market just south of us. A 2005 issue of the indie magazine *Under the Radar* dedicated thirty-plus pages to Canadian musicians—Tegan and Sara included. Mark Redfern proclaimed in his editor's letter for the issue that "it's hard to dispute that there have been a lot of exciting Canadian indie-rock bands creeping over the border in the last few years." He was also cognizant to add that they'd cast a big net over the Canadian acts gaining attention, and that they "may not all share a singular sound."[30]

It was around that time that the international press—from gatekeepers like *Rolling Stone* to emerging tastemakers like *Pitchfork*, *Drowned in Sound*, and *Stereogum*—began turning to Canada for its musical offerings. And it was 2004 that cemented Canada—especially Montreal, which was christened that year as the "next big music scene" by *Spin Magazine*[31]—as a musical hotspot, stealing the spotlight from US cities like New York City or Seattle that had been strongholds for decades. A year later, the *New York Times* affirmed Canada's influence by declaring that "you can hear music with a Montreal address on any radio in America."[32] James Keast points out how rare it is for concentrated music scenes like this to emerge, noting the '90s Halifax scene and Montreal as two exceptions to the rule. "In Canada, it's kind of an unusual thing to happen," he says.

While acts like the Dears, Stars, and more were credited with helping to light the fuse, the early 2000s Montreal indie-rock explosion mostly focused on one breakout act: Arcade Fire. The band, led by Texas native Win Butler and his Montreal-born partner Regine Chassagne, was heralded by *Time Magazine* as "the world's most intriguing rock band" and attracted A-list fans like David Bowie and David Byrne.[33] Their debut album, *Funeral*, is currently the seventh highest-selling indie album of all time, according to Music Canada.[34] It's easy to see how Arcade Fire's success cast a long shadow on other acts in Montreal—or Canada in general. But that shadow felt especially impossible for Tegan and Sara to avoid; coincidentally, they released their fourth studio album, *So Jealous*, on the exact same day as *Funeral*.

Pitchfork ended its *Funeral* review (which received a rare, near perfect 9.7 rating) with a bold declaration: "It's taken perhaps too long for us to reach this point where an album is at least capable of completely and successfully restoring the tainted phrase 'emotion' to its true origin." *NME* praised it as the "most cathartic album of the year." However, publications were a little less kind to Tegan and Sara, furthering an already sour relationship between the Quin sisters and critics. By comparison, *So Jealous* got a less than fifty-word writeup in Spin Magazine's October 2004 issue. Sandwiched next to two other bite-sized reviews, more than a third of the word count was taken up by this opening remark: "Lesbians, sisters, and proud Canucks, this duo was once a Wicca-folk nightmare."[35]

Ganz remembers that short but memorable blurb and assures me that the writer, Jon Dolan (now an editor at *Rolling Stone*), "would be completely horrified if he knew that: a) he had said that, and b) that it has endured in culture and for [Tegan and Sara]." For all the momentum that the internet was gaining, Ganz is steadfast in her assertion that no one at *Spin Magazine*—a publication that published its last print edition in 2012—was thinking about the online legacy of its writing at the time. "The sense of distance you had from the subjects you were writing about was massive," she explains.

"So it was a lot easier to write something nasty about somebody and be like, 'Well whatever, it's in print. Who cares?' It's not like they're going to tweet at you, right? They're not going to email you. There was no dialogue; you couldn't have a meaningful back and forth."

This isn't to excuse the phrase "Wicca-folk nightmare"—it sits up there as one of the most prominent labels attached to Tegan and Sara, like a scarlet letter—but it speaks to the "zingy" style, as described by Ganz, of writing that was key to the casual, cool culture of magazines like *Spin* or *Blender*. "There was an edit comment at *Spin* that was like a joke that we all got—it was 'make funnier,'" Ganz recalls. "So you'd write something and you get a bunch of 'make funniers' on it and you'd be like, [sigh] alright fine. You'd punch it up like you're a late-show writer."

But *So Jealous*, divorced from its divisive reception in the press, actually unlocked an entirely new world of opportunities and success for the sisters. *So Jealous* took *If It Was You*'s foundation and built a skyscraper on top of it. The goal was to craft hooks that were bigger and better, for Tegan and Sara to push themselves in both the rock and pop spectrums of their sound. It was a mammoth undertaking that, quite frankly, they took on not because they wanted to chase fame or become big pop stars, but for pure survival.

The year leading up to the recording of *So Jealous*, Sara recalled making just $21,000. "I was living fairly artistically and under the radar, but I was also a grownup," she reflected in an *Under the Radar* interview in 2014, on the album's tenth anniversary. "I was thinking, at some point I'm probably going to have to be realistic; either I'm going to do this on the side and have a job, or I'm going to have this as my job. So there was a real thrust forward."[36]

During this time, Sara made one of the biggest decisions in her and the band's existence: she moved to Montreal, away from Tegan for the first time in their lives. "If I'd stayed in Vancouver, the band wouldn't have survived," she states, disclosing how unhappy she felt there. A desire for space wasn't Sara signifying the end of the band, though—she was eager to grow in ways that could benefit herself and her music. But that's not how Tegan saw it. For Tegan, hearing that her sister wanted to move across the country sparked anger, which she now acknowledges was just "thinly veiled fear." Tegan thought Sara was running off to Montreal and saddling her with more work, as Tegan already handled most of the band's business affairs, from meeting with managers to all the banking. In her resentful reaction, Tegan had failed to take Sara's emotional state into account, but soon concern shifted to more pragmatic matters. How were they going to share their MacBook tower? (This was a time before cloud storage.) Should Sara purchase a cell phone to stay in touch? How would they rehearse? "I was really stuck in the weeds about the details," Tegan says now. In hindsight, Sara understands all of her sister's apprehensions. "Our relationship was in a terrible place, so why wouldn't you think, we're so fucked?"

Sara didn't even know if returning to the west coast would ever be a possibility, given the band's financial situation. But almost immediately, Montreal provided the reinvigoration she needed. In search of a younger and more creative environment, Sara quickly flung herself into the midst of the city's burgeoning music scene. Bands that Sara often name-checks from her early years there—Arcade Fire, the Stills, the Dears—were all kick-starting their careers around the time of her arrival. Guitar-rock dominated the sound, but it was expressed in a number of electrifying ways, whether it was the orchestral-backed pop-rock of the Dears and Stars or the gargantuan anthems of collectives like Arcade Fire and Toronto's Broken Social Scene. The sound and scene that Tegan and Sara began tapping into during *If It Was You* was rapidly becoming a blueprint for many bands across the country. "Almost immediately, she started writing songs," Tegan says of Sara. "I think right away I was like, 'Oh, Montreal was a good thing.'" In time, Sara's output motivated Tegan to start writing too.

One of the first songs Sara wrote for the album, which turned out to be *So Jealous*' biggest single, was "Walking with a Ghost," a deceptively simple song that only consists of a pre-chorus and chorus. Songwriting rules often dictate a need for verses or bridges to give a chorus some breathing room. But, partly influenced by the music of unconventional songwriters like Brian Eno, "Walking with a Ghost" cycles back and forth between two interchangeable parts; Sara's voice clashes against the song's acoustic and electric guitar parts—later

fleshed out with synths hovering in the background—
and an atypical drum part that came from a mistake in
timing by Rob Chursinoff in rehearsal and was kept in by
the producers. Inspired by walks Sara would take in her
new city, imagining she was with a person she wanted to
date ("Some would call it an imaginary friend; I call it
a ghost," she explained to MTV in 2004[37]), the cyclical
nature of "Walking with a Ghost," along with other songs
that would appear on *So Jealous*, felt like a practice in
manifesting, or convincing oneself of, something, a common coping mechanism for dealing with monumental
life change. "No matter which way you go/ No matter
which way you stay/ You're out of my mind, out of my
mind/ Out of my mind, out of my mind," Sara sings,
shifting the weight of her words to emphasize "out" the
first time and "my" the second as if it's a phrase she's
chewing on in hopes of landing on a version that would
ultimately sound true coming out of her mouth.

While Sara was adjusting to her new living environment, Tegan's life remained the same on the surface.
But she, too, was battling discomfort and unfamiliar territory. Having gotten accustomed to touring for months
at a time, the idea of being at home felt uneasy for Tegan,
who was in a very long and complicated relationship
with a woman in Vancouver during the time between
If It Was You and *So Jealous*. "I didn't know how to be
normal: how to fit in, how to take care of a home, how
to take care of someone other than myself," she wrote in
So Jealous X, a book that accompanied the album's tenth
anniversary edition. This didn't stop Tegan's creativ-

ity, though. It fuelled it. In the span of one weekend in Vancouver, Tegan wrote three songs that ended up on *So Jealous*: "Take Me Anywhere," "I Know I Know I Know," and "Where Does the Good Go."

In 2014, Tegan told *Spin Magazine* that "Take Me Anywhere" was "the beginning of me trying to write a basic pop song,"[38] following a path that she'd already set out on in the previous album, whether she was aware of it or not. "I Know I Know I Know" employs repetition in a different way than "Walking with a Ghost," using the repeated refrain of its title only in the chorus to hammer home a heart-on-sleeve plea to live in the moment, to weather changes along with a loved one. The chorus is two lines, as direct and straightforward as can be; in relationships, sometimes things need to be communicated clearly and directly in order to have the biggest impact.

"Where Does the Good Go" completes the trifecta of songs that came out of that writing session. An acoustic number that grows into a swelling tambourine-assisted chorus, Tegan frames love as a well into which you can pour all your happiness. But when that love ends, after all your hopes of happiness and strength have been funnelled into this one place, she asks, plainly, "Where do you go with your broken heart in tow?/ What do you do with the leftover you?"

Collins and Carswell returned as producers on *So Jealous*; producer Howard Redekopp joined them to offset the pair's busy schedule, which included gigs with the New Pornographers and the Evaporators. Another person who came into the fold around this time was Matt Sharp, the former bassist and one of the founding members of Weezer, as well as leader of the Rentals; he'd fallen in love with Tegan and Sara's music after he was randomly handed a copy of *If It Was You* by his publicist. Feeling so moved by the record, he toured briefly with Tegan and Sara near the end of that record cycle; their live set-up at the time was missing a keyboardist and he offered to perform. Many note Sharp as a pivotal addition to the *So Jealous* recording process, contributing more Moog and keyboards to the album than was asked of him, but Collins says that helped push the band's sound forward, even toward a more new-wave sound. "I just wanted to do whatever I could for them at that point," Sharp gushes. "So I wrote, I don't know, twelve song parts for like, twelve songs instead of two or three, or whatever it was. I basically said, 'You can use as much or as little as you want.'" The majority of his offerings stayed in, including a subtle but dreamy background part whirling on Sara's acoustic number, "Downtown."

"He loved all the keyboard ideas we'd already recorded," Tegan notes, adding that Sharp's approval reaffirmed the more keyboard-heavy direction they took. Tegan says some of that merit also goes to Collins and Carswell: "I think the New Pornographers were actually kind of ahead of their time, and so we knew this was where music was going—that it was going to have a lot of melodic keyboard instrumentation." That instinct proved correct as even more rock acts—like the Killers, the Postal Service, and Metric—embraced synths.

The record gets its name from a song Sara penned. An air organ throbs throughout both the "So Jealous" demo and final version, something Redekopp says made him feel seasick the first time he heard it, with the organ expanding and taking up space with each repeated note. Pushing back are Sara's vocals, five takes layered on top of one another to amplify her frustration as she shouts on the chorus: "I want the ocean right now/ I get so jealous I can't even work." That moment explodes, musically, like a wave crashing. It's thunderous, cacophonous, and, honestly, it's ugly. But that's what jealousy is: it's often painted as shameful to give in to desires, to compare oneself to someone or something else. As the crux of the album, the song encapsulates a raw and messy energy that courses through each track. More specifically, "So Jealous" captures that outsider sensation Sara felt so intensely while witnessing bands around her in Montreal take off. In the studio, Sara told Tegan, as recalled in their 2014 *Spin Magazine* interview: "I think it would be really funny to call the record *So Jealous*." Tegan wondered if she meant this in jest, but Sara responded, "It's not a joke to me. I am jealous. I am so jealous."[39]

That's what makes *So Jealous* feel human and relatable. Those thoughts—Sara categorizes the ocean line in particular as a tantrum—might seem juvenile to some people, but that emotional mayhem doesn't escape adulthood. In fact, it only gets worse. These songs, revisited many years later, resonate more or less, but each listen still unravels new layers. In another ten-year anniversary interview with *Time Magazine*, Sara herself describes how she feels revisiting the songs on *So Jealous* a decade later: "Oh my God, we were being really dramatic!"[40]

Tegan and Sara are credited on *So Jealous* as co-producers, something that didn't happen on *If It Was You*, though Collins would argue it's a title they should've had then, too. Producing is one of the many jobs Tegan and Sara—and young women artists in general—take on in the studio, but credits are often stripped, whether in liner note titles or in the press. This is because behind-the-scenes roles have historically been an even more male-dominated field than being front and centre as an artist. In a 2021 study published by USC Annenberg, which looked at 600 of the top songs on the *Billboard* charts between 2012 and 2020, the ratio of male to female producers was 38 to 1.[41] In a lot of cases, female producers' work has either been overshadowed by men over the years or completely erased by history.

"The demos of our songs played such a bigger role," Tegan says of both *If It Was You* and *So Jealous*. "We had such a heavy, heavy influence on what our music sounded like, and we played everything. We were in the studio every single second giving feedback… I think it's actually something in our industry that isn't widely talked about, and I think women especially end up suffering because of that."

After the release of *So Jealous*, Tegan and Sara scored an opening slot for the Killers, a Las Vegas band that was one of the hottest acts at the time thanks to their explosive debut, *Hot Fuss*. Though his memory of discovering Tegan and Sara's music is cloudy now, drummer Ronnie Vannuci Jr. remembers their voices having "this quality to them, and a quality to ['Walking with a Ghost'] that was equal parts cool, and new, and exciting." He was also impressed by Tegan and Sara's professionalism on the road. "We were both sort of zygotes in our career, but they seemed further along," he mentions. "They had a routine and we were still figuring out when bedtime was, and things like that, so in some ways they might've been mentors to us." The Killers' guitarist Dave Keuning was so impressed by Tegan and Sara's opening sets that he continued buying Tegan and Sara's albums in the years following their first tour together: "They made a believer out of me just from that one tour."

It was on that tour that Tegan, Sara, and their bandmates noticed an uptick in success that felt substantial. In the middle of that Killers tour, Tegan and Sara crossed the 50,000 album sales benchmark, a massive marker for a band of their size. "Oh my God, 50,000 is like a million to me," Sara told *Under the Radar Magazine* in 2014. "Up to that point, it felt like we had to sell every CD ourselves. It was like, one...two...three. To me, 50,000 signalled, 'Okay, it's out of our hands. We're not in charge of all of this now.'"[42] By then, "Walking with a Ghost" had caught on with college radio stations, and Chursinoff remembers the crowd recognition of that single was almost immediate, as early as the band's second stop with the Killers. "When we started playing that song, the crowd—which was definitely a Killers crowd—knew it and they started cheering. We kind of looked around and we were like, 'Oh, the crowd knows us! That really energized us."

Around that same time, Tegan and Sara also played the 2005 Coachella Valley Music and Arts Festival. They were scheduled after the Fiery Furnaces and before Arcade Fire. "I remember thinking, 'Oh, this is where I wanna be, I love these bands,'" Sara says. On the flip side, she also felt haunted by Arcade Fire's parallel success. "Everything that happened with *So Jealous*—I always compared it to what was happening to *Funeral*. I just remember so much in those couple of years after *So Jealous* came out, just being completely preoccupied with what was happening in their career."

"Now I have a total sense of humour about it, but back then Tegan would just be like, 'Who gives a shit about Arcade Fire? Can't you just like them and not compare us to them?' And I'd be like, *I want what they have. I feel like I'd be happier if we had what Arcade Fire had.* Here I was at the epicentre, where it seemed like every band was exploding and cool, and it was impossible for me to not feel like we were being left out of it. I couldn't tell if it was because we were gay or because we didn't have that cool factor. And yet, I think in a lot of those cases we were actually bigger and more successful than [those Montreal bands]. But I still felt like we were invisible, you know?"

Even though the Montreal scene didn't share a singular sound, it did share an ethos forged through community and collaboration. This was a factor that presented a barrier for Sara, who almost exclusively works with her sister. "I remember Wolf Parade and Arcade Fire being like a sprawling, messy, ramshackle scene," Sarah Liss says, referring to both those bands' raucous, DIY sounds and the effort it took to keep track of overlapping members and projects coming out of the city. As a duo, and a band with a more polished, pop-minded sound, Tegan and Sara's trajectory was always more self-contained. Vannucci offers a counter perspective by suggesting that no one truly fits into any scene and arguing that scenes are the narrativization tactics of media outlets. "Fitting in isn't what it's all about," he says. "It's like fucking *Lord of the Flies* out there, everybody's trying to make it and they're stepping on each other's heads to get to the top." Collins, a musician who, depending on who was describing the Montreal scene, could've been considered part of it, laughs now and concedes: "I don't even know what the Canadian indie-rock scene is, to be honest." He jokes that his awareness of other bands at that time was fairly low given how much he kept his head down to focus on his own work.

Outside of their opening act bubble, increased radio play also helped Tegan and Sara reach new audiences, including young women and LGBTQ+ fans who were witnessing, maybe for the first time, artists who looked like them, who were unconventional (i.e. not femme), alternative, queer. While Tegan and Sara weren't shy about their sexuality, they weren't terribly outspoken during this time about their identity politics, conveying much of their queerness through the way they styled their hair or their clothes. Of course, Tegan and Sara's

LGBTQ+ following has existed for years, but Sara says she didn't fully realize just how much they had cultivated a queer fanbase until headlining one show in Texas, where she remembers "setting up the merch and opening the doors, and everyone was a fan."

"Like, it wasn't a big crowd, it was probably only twenty or thirty people," she continues, "but I remember thinking, we have a crowd now. We're building an audience. It wasn't necessarily that it was women, but it was that they looked more like us: they had mullets, they had zip-up American Apparel hoodies and T-shirts." Gradually, the LGBTQ+ portion of their audience became more reflective of the type of queerness Tegan and Sara represented. For lack of better phrasing, Sara calls it "the stripey shirt" faction, referencing the rather common uniform she and Tegan sported around this time. "[These fans] were looking for striped shirts, too!"

This stood out as monumental for Sara, especially as bands were still in the early stages of learning how to use the internet for their own personal and promotional purposes. Back then, arriving in a city for a gig was a crap shoot. Bands, if unfamiliar with a stop, were unsure of who or what might greet them, and scouting out queer-friendly spaces, shops, or even just a good bookstore was hard to do before smartphones. So when Tegan and Sara spotted fans that looked like them it was a huge relief. This was proof that their music was understood and embraced outside their inner circle, and that they weren't alone—a mutually gratifying feeling for both artist and fan. And with show sizes still relatively small, the space between Tegan, Sara, and their audiences felt paper thin. In an effort to understand this connection more, I wanted to speak with queer Tegan and Sara fans and specifically asked them about their unique experiences connecting with the band live. Laura Campbell, a super-fan I met through a mutual friend, explained to me how their concerts helped develop an even stronger bond between her and them as artists. "There's something about the ability to make believe in your head that you're able to make a connection with an artist—that makes all the difference," she tells me. "They were real people who've had similar experiences to what I had."

Campbell saw Tegan and Sara for the first time during their Canadian *So Jealous* tour and says it was the "first place where I walked in and really felt like there was a connection with my space, and I hadn't felt that as a queer person before." She wells up thinking back to this profound memory, noting that the incredible concert itself served as a bonus on top of the towering feeling of acceptance she got from just being in the room. And she wasn't alone. This is a sensation felt by many new Tegan and Sara fans as their music disseminated throughout North America and beyond, thanks to the increased radio play and support from online spaces. The internet in general became a crucial arena for queer music enthusiasts to find music that reflected their lived experiences and offered opportunities to connect with other likeminded fans. For example, fan and aforementioned University of Southern California lecturer Chris Belcher describes stumbling on Tegan and Sara as an internet discovery. "I came out into a world that was very much either Melissa Etheridge or Indigo Girls," they explained. "But I was looking for lesbian musicians who were closer to my age or my tastes."

Headlining also allowed Tegan and Sara to be more curatorial with their opening acts. For example, during their *So Jealous* tour in the US, they brought a then up-and-comer named Vivek Shraya on tour with them. Shraya, who grew up in Edmonton, just three hours north of Tegan and Sara's hometown of Calgary, moved to Toronto in the early 2000s to pursue a career in music. During a 2003 Tegan and Sara show at Lee's Palace, Shraya threw one of her CDs—on which she'd scrawled her email address and phone number—up on stage, narrowly missing Tegan's head. A month later, Shraya received an email "basically saying that they get all kinds of music when they're on the road, but that they were really moved by my CD and they'd be happy to do anything they could to support me." Soon after, Tegan and Sara posted Shraya's music on their website. The following year, she joined them on tour. "They'd never seen me play before," Shraya adds. "They invited me based on their faith in my music. The support from another artist actually in some ways is more valuable than support from an agent or a manager—like, what they have done is single-handedly give me a career."

All that touring helped Tegan and Sara grow their profile, and soon awards attention was also trickling in. *So Jealous* netted Tegan and Sara their first Juno Award nomination for alternative album of the year in 2006, narrowly missing the 2005 submission period in which Arcade Fire's *Funeral* was nominated. Tegan and Sara ultimately lost to Broken Social Scene's 2005 self-titled release. But in all honesty, the Junos, and the Canadian music industry by extension, had fallen down the sisters' priority list. When asked if the Juno nomination that year meant anything, Tegan is quick to say no. "Nothing. It meant nothing. Sales meant a lot to us," she emphasized, "and going gold was a very exciting moment, but by the time we got nominated for a Juno, we had been fucking trudging it out already for eight years. Back then, I was like—we did Letterman, we did Leno—we were just indignant."

Sara's most meaningful marker of success wasn't tied to awards either. "My grandmother never put anything on her fridge—she was a very clean, almost sterile person—but she cut out our review from *Rolling Stone* and put it on her refrigerator. I remember being in disbelief, but she was really proud! It was a significant cultural marker that she understood."

Then came the primetime TV show spots. Between April and October 2005, Tegan and Sara landed seven songs on Shonda Rhimes' breakout ABC hit, *Grey's Anatomy*, a medical drama that quickly grew a reputation for giving indie artists a platform thanks to music supervisor Alexandra Patsavas, who also worked on hit teen dramas *The O.C.* and *Gossip Girl*.[43] Patsavas helped launch artists like Snow Patrol, Death Cab for Cutie, and the Killers by featuring their songs on shows that were racking up millions of viewers on a weekly basis—a fertile ground for acts who would otherwise only reach hundreds, or maybe thousands, of listeners on their own. At the time, music supervisors were just as vital to artists as publicists, and landing a song on a show or commercial was becoming the new goal post for success. This was far from the days of being accused of selling out, as drastic changes in the music industry were in the process of destabilizing artists' incomes. With the internet shifting the way artists and labels made money—file sharing and illegal downloading rendered album sales nearly obsolete—TV, film, and commercials provided a profitable income stream. And in many cases, instead of paying up for legacy artists, up-and-coming musicians were given the chance to shine at a more reasonable price point.

"We were still fairly broke," Sara remembers, "so it's hard to say no to enough money that I could put a down payment on a condo. Which was something that, as a twenty-five-year-old, I felt pressure to do." In addition to *Grey's Anatomy*, Tegan and Sara's music was also heavily highlighted on one of network television's most influential and groundbreaking queer shows, *The L Word*. The show, which many praised for challenging and changing the television landscape when queer representation was scarce and mostly focused on gay men, helped many queer women embrace their sexuality by creating characters that were well-rounded as opposed to stereotyped. The show's music supervisor, Natasha Duprey, had been pushing to feature Tegan and Sara's music since the beginning of the series in January 2004, but finally found a spot for it in its third season. "Every song on *So Jealous* is a gem," Duprey says, noting Tegan and Sara's onscreen cameo in the episode "Last Dance" as a personal highlight of the third season.

By the end of 2005, Tegan and Sara would get another substantial boost from an unlikely source: rock duo the White Stripes. In November 2005, the Detroit band—who had by then performed at the MTV Video Music Awards, earned a Brit Award and gained worldwide acclaim for songs like "Fell in Love with a Girl" and "Seven Nation Army"—released a cover of "Walking with a Ghost." Jack and Meg White's take replaced Tegan and Sara's acoustic arrangement with a searing electric one, with instruments loudly reverberating in the forefront as Jack's voice squeaks underneath the weight of his guitar and Meg's shivering cymbals.

Given the White Stripes' worldwide popularity, the cover had an immense impact on Tegan and Sara's career—it was a red, white, and black-striped cherry on top of the sundae *So Jealous* proved to be, commercially. It was arguably even more influential for Tegan and Sara's career than signing to Vapor Records. "I think post-Hayden, people had immediately grown skeptical of Neil Young's ability to shepherd in new talent," Keast argues. "He didn't demonstrate an immediate golden touch." The White Stripes, on the other hand, were at the centre of the rock universe in the early 2000s, and to get roped into their orbit meant reaping the many rewards of their popularity.

Despite the tangible evidence that Tegan and Sara were growing into a bigger, more notable force, reviews were more divisive than ever. Again, many reviews were actually positive, but heavyweight publications like *Pitchfork* and *NME*, which were known for breaking or making new artists, cast a dark cloud over *So Jealous'* critical reputation with harsh reviews. *Pitchfork*, who awarded Arcade Fire's *Funeral* a Best New Music label just a few months prior, slapped *So Jealous* with a 3.4 in January 2005.

"The first single from *So Jealous*, 'Walking with a Ghost,' sounds like one of those dummy MP3s major labels post on Kazaa to fool unsuspecting music lovers, where the first ten seconds loop for five minutes," senior staff writer Marc Hogan wrote. "'Walking with a Ghost' repeats three or four mundane phrases—particularly 'out of my mind'—dozens of times in two-and-a-half minutes, all over the same jerky, studio-polished guitar chords. I suppose it's almost as catchy as the latest McDonalds jingle, but it's also utterly boring."[44] At the end of the year, *Pitchfork* retreaded this criticism in their review of the White Stripes' *Walking with a Ghost* EP; writer Matthew Murphy expressed bewilderment over the band's choice to cover Tegan and Sara: "Those who find Tegan and Sara's skeletal brand of winsome Canadian pop to be unbearably trite and/or mundane will presumably remain unswayed by the White Stripes' modest Detroit upgrade."[45] That EP received a 6.1 rating.

While *Pitchfork*'s review—like many others that both praised and panned the album—slid toward sexist narratives or remarks (for example, giving extra weight to Collins and Carswell's contributions even though Tegan and Sara had co-producer credits), *NME* made their misogyny crystal clear: "Quite lovely, even if they do hate cock."[46] Even in that zippy era of edgy writing, it was a review that completely missed the mark.

At that point, most of Tegan and Sara's team was comprised of men, which meant the sisters' particular struggles didn't completely register for anyone else. Chursinoff is honest about his lack of awareness: "I did not fully understand the microaggressions; I wasn't tuned into it at the time. Apart from, like, Melissa Ethridge, there weren't a lot of gay icons, especially not in indie-rock, so I think the press was still trying to figure out how to talk about them. I didn't always get it, and how could I? It was a big learning experience and we tried to have their backs." But, he adds, these experiences also "toughened them up."

Despite their rise in stature, Sara was unable to shake the bitter aftertaste of the demeaning language that permeated most of the press around their music. Additionally, both the Montreal and Toronto music scenes felt like enmeshed communities that Sara and her sister couldn't penetrate. "I wanted to fit in, but the signals made me feel like we weren't fitting in," she says. "We weren't popular with the people I saw as gatekeepers in that world, even though I thought we were in the right place."

PART 3:
BALANCE

TEGAN AND SARA HAVE ALWAYS STRIVED FOR EQUILIBRIUM. Their personalities are yin and yang: Sara is prone to give in to her anxieties and darkness, while Tegan can almost always claw her way out of the grips of those dispiriting black holes in search of a silver lining. Tegan illustrates their interconnection with her hands over Zoom, holding each one up like a seesaw constantly in motion: "It's always been like this. This has been our success."

Coming off the high of *So Jealous'* success, that seesaw struggled to find its balance. As Sara settled into a stable relationship in Montreal, Tegan found herself getting out of one. Then tragedy struck: their grandmother, who had been an integral figure and caretaker of theirs growing up, died. That prized *Rolling Stone* review she'd hung on her pristine refrigerator was the last album of Tegan and Sara's she would ever hear. And then, during the writing process for their next record, their longtime lawyer also died.

Death and grief dominated the themes of their fifth studio album, *The Con*. If *So Jealous* dove headfirst into the messiness of everyday relationships, *The Con* amplified the fear and anxiety of relationships that cycle between obsessive and debilitating, a loop of trepidation. *The Con* is arguably one of Tegan and Sara's most cherished albums by fans—it's my personal favourite—and perhaps the most knotty gateway for newcomers. The album is densely packed and contains interlocking parts that, as Tegan told NPR in 2017, in retrospect, break "all the rules of music theory." Case in point: a decade after its release, Tegan and Sara's musical director tried to assess the arrangements for a live performance and reported back with "The record is a mess."[47]

But the album's producer, former Death Cab For Cutie guitarist Chris Walla, points out that the main draw is the sheer range of emotion, something that comes off so clearly in Tegan and Sara's performances of the songs. "They're just so desperate," Walla says, meaning it as a compliment. "They have so much feeling." *The Con* is a natural stepping stone in the band's progression. Sonically, it takes picks up from where *So Jealous* left off, but it's more complex—a challenge that Tegan and Sara were committed to taking on for personal and professional growth. "I think a lot of people thought we would go into the studio and make *So Jealous* part two, or aim for another 'Walking with a Ghost,'" Tegan says. "And we had no intention of doing that."

"We were gonna make a bigger album and we were going to keep going in the direction we'd been going in," Sara says, noting that her and Tegan's visions were very much aligned. Heading into Walla's home studio in Portland, Tegan, Sara, and Walla decided to record everything backward, ending with drums and bass instead of starting with them. This allowed the sisters to hew closer to their experimental demos and control the sound even more than on their previous records. "I just remember the first few weeks being really open and collaborative," Walla recalls. Walla was one in a string of producers who encouraged Tegan and Sara's oddities, leaning into the unique ways they approached playing music. "He's just not, like, the take-the-guitar-out-of-your-hand-and-do-it-for-you kind of guy," Tegan says. "He's like, 'No, you do it really cool and weird, so keep doing that.' And I like that."

The album kicks off with Sara's "I Was Married." One of the most stripped-back and bare songs of the album's total fourteen, it is also one of the most thematically powerful and overtly political in an otherwise fairly unpolitical discography. While Tegan and Sara's identities have been politicized by external forces since the outset, their earlier music has mostly steered clear from overt statement-making. Over an echoing piano and guitar riff that beam like a sunrise, on "I Was Married," Sara sings of a bigger force trying to control same-sex relationships.

In 2006, the US was still under President Bush's administration and the country was still nine years away from legalizing same-sex marriage. Although Sara is a Canadian citizen and same-sex marriage was by then legal in her home country, her partner (and the band's art director since 2003) Emy Storey is American. After years of living together in Montreal, Storey decided to apply to become a permanent resident. The only two options available were for Sara and Storey to get married or go to city hall and declare their common-law status. They opted for the latter. The appointment felt almost like a wedding ceremony anyway, and that angered Sara. She recalls riding away with Storey on their bikes and just burning with rage instead of relishing the moment: "It sounds so stupid and big, but I remember just leaving and being like, 'I fucking hate the patriarchy!' I hate that we have to prove this to people. I hate that the system isn't set up for us."

Even though *The Con*'s album opener is a tender, delicate moment—Sara says the original composition was much more cluttered, full of rhythmic guitar parts that she later muted and removed—it's fuelled by a caustic disapproval of the societal structures that work against LGBTQ+ people. Fans noticed that the sisters' queerness on the album was more explicit, and many were thrilled to see them embrace it. As a teenager who perhaps didn't pay the most attention to Tegan and Sara's sexuality at first, I began to consider with *The Con* how beging gay informed not only their personalities, but their songwriting, in a way that deepened by love for them. When looking back at why fans related so much to their more open approach to their queerness, Sara told cultural critic Karen Tongson in a 2021 livestreamed Q&A: "It was the first album that I think we got out of the boundary of love. The songs are not necessarily about romantic love; they're sort of about something bigger than that. There's a sort of unique footprint, or whatever you want to call it— the way we see the world as queer people. We didn't sound like straight girls who were contemplating grief and death, we sounded like gay girls contemplating grief and death."[48] Sara says the years around *The Con* felt like the right time to really assert themselves more politically, and it showed in the interviews they did after the album's release. Current events drove them to try, as Sara says, to integrate their "personal politics into not just our music, but into the landscape of the music industry." While defending *The Con* in CBC's *Canada Listens* competition in 2021, writer Alicia Elliott noted: "[It] hides its revolution in plain sight."[49]

————

If Tegan and Sara previously appeared timid around the topic of their sexuality and the politics surrounding LGBTQ+ issues, *The Con* marked a turning point. Prop 8 and the fight to legalize gay marriage fuelled the sisters to speak out more publicly. For Sara, the hesitation to be more active in the public discourse stemmed from a fear of having those conversations with people she wasn't close to. "It's just hard not to feel like every conversation about our sexuality was balanced on the edge of a knife," Sara explains. "Whether it was in interviews, or it was in a taxi cab, or with some guy in a bar, it just felt like, at any point, the conversation could go to a place that I didn't want it to go, and I think that always made me feel cagey."

Sarah Liss says this openness was significant for Tegan and Sara's fans; it was "like a shift into advocacy in a particular way and a shift into being icons in a particular way." But both sisters continued to feel a small sense of denial that they'd cultivated a significant queer following. Tegan argues that the clear markers—doing gay press, touring with many LGBTQ+ acts—hadn't really happened for them. She jokes that she wasn't staring out into the crowd at live shows and counting gay people—"I can't fucking see anything" due to the blinding stage lights —and concedes that journalists probably had a better sense of the crowd's makeup at their concerts. And Liss can attest to the queer spaces Tegan and Sara created; recalling their headlining show at Toronto's Danforth Music Hall for the tour behind *The Con*, Liss says, "I just remember every lesbian I knew was there [...] There was something very much like, 'They are ours, and we are owning them.'"

Once "I Was Married" wraps, the rest of the album kicks in with bigger, more anthemic sounds that amp up the indie-rock intensity. On "The Con," a track that Tegan and Sara renamed to match the album title (its original was "Encircle Me"), a confessional start that's paired with acoustic strumming revs up until a dam breaks open, inviting in synths, bass, drums, and harmonies to amplify Tegan's feelings of melodrama—she admits, "Nobody likes to but I really like to cry / Nobody likes me, maybe if I cry." Drums on tracks like "The Con," "Are You Ten Years Ago?", and "Nineteen" are massive, almost Phil Collins-esque in scale. That's thanks to Death Cab For Cutie's Jason McGerr, brought on board by Walla to replace Chursinoff, who exited the band around this time. "We were on the route to not getting along, and not being friends," Chursinoff admits, looking back at

Tegan and Sara's decision to let him go. It's something he appears grateful for today, as they've managed to remain friends in the years since.

Even though "The Con" bears the album's name, another of Tegan's tracks, "Nineteen," feels like the true beating heart of the album. Charged with a big '80s drum sound, the song hits the peak of that desperation Walla described, showing Tegan at her most helplessly romantic. Her voice pushes past her comfort zone, as if the extra stretch will reach across the country to her long-distance crush, the subject of most of her songs on the album.

Walla was really psyched about the big drum break-down on the track's climax during recording, but now he looks back with some contrition, partly because of his own ability as an engineer at the time. "'Nineteen' sounds lazy," he says, with a mix of chagrin and regret. "It's kind of really dense, it's kind of claustrophobic. The drums, in my memory, feel like they're almost in the next room. It's really weird." Of course, Walla is nitpick-ing at what actually makes that song work—a distance that may have been a misfire for him ends up giving the subject matter of the song so much more depth in the end. "Tegan sang the shit out of that song, certainly because she was feeling it in there, but I think it was also in part because what she was listening to in her head was so aggressive," Walla says of the analog approach to recording the album, which led to headphone mixes sounding perhaps heavier than he intended. "It's disor-ganized and unruly, and pretty wild."

With both sisters landing seven songs each on this album—a first, given that previous albums leaned heavier into Tegan's compositions—Tegan and Sara also enlisted their touring guitarist and keyboardist Ted Gowans to help out in the studio, as well as two bassists—AFI's Hunter Burgan on Tegan's tracks and Matt Sharp returning to play on Sara's.

Sharp upped his contributions from what he calls the "textures" he added on *So Jealous* to a more prominent role on *The Con* for songs like "Back in Your Head" and "Like O, Like H." Sharp himself was going through a rough time, feeling stuck in a "deep, dark black void." He almost didn't make the trip to Portland to record, but Sara demanded that he show up, convincing him that being in the studio might help him work through his depressive state. "It was probably the most meaningful thing that's happened to me," he tells me, stating his true pride in the work he ended up doing on the record. "I haven't been in that dark place since."

Lightning struck on *So Jealous*, and it somehow struck a second time when the sisters entered the studio for *The Con*. After achieving more commercial than critical success with their last release, *The Con* expanded Tegan and Sara's visibility in the indie world, a win for a band that wanted to assert themselves as an indie-rock force. The album eventually began to forge a path into the emo and hardcore scenes; their music's emotional intensity found a kindred spirit in fans of more aggressive rock, an arena that has historically been very male-dominated in both its acts and its fanbase.

Toronto hardcore band Cancer Bats covered Tegan and Sara's "So Jealous" in 2007. Lead singer Liam Cormier says it was important at the time to show their community that "it was okay to be into whatever you wanted. Just cause you like punk doesn't mean you can't be into Tegan and Sara." Cormier's Tegan and Sara fandom only grew stronger when *The Con* came out: "I thought it was an amazing album. At no point did they play it safe. You could tell they were trying to push themselves as musicians and artists. I felt, as an artist, that this was exactly what I needed at the time: they were an example of true punk spirit as artists not giving a shit about anything but the art in front of them that they were making." Jenn Pelly notes that this kinship between Tegan and Sara and the emo scene makes sense because they were both maligned in the press for similar reasons. "The vulnerability of [Tegan and Sara's] music was probably not considered cool," she says, "in the same way a lot of emo and pop-punk wasn't considered cool."

The Con ends on "Call it Off," a song that Walla says just spilled out of Tegan. "It was just so effortless and seamless." The final version that makes it on the record is either the first or second take Tegan recorded in Walla's studio. After an album that, for the most part, goes in circles, indulging in compulsive repetition that spins itself into a frenzy many times over—a quality that lures in some and loses others—"Call it Off" feels like a pressure valve being released. It signals the end of a relationship that, in reality, sparked the beginning of a five-year romance with the very person Tegan was mourning. *The Con*'s cyclical nature, both in its overall cinematic arc and on individual songs, is transfixing. It's dark and neurotic ("The labour of pining for someone is very addictive," Tegan admits), but isn't it comforting to indulge in darkness sometimes? It's an album about beginnings and endings, resolutions and possibilities—it celebrates those transitional periods that can feel turbulent but can be soothed by the perfect score. For many of Tegan and Sara's most devoted fans, this album became their soundtrack. In an Instagram story, author Hanif Abdurraqib wrote, "*The Con* is such an elite heartbreak/breakup album like an album that totally rewired how I cope with that specific kind of ache, that signaled to me that I could feel, like, twelve different things at once from second to second."

The high of writing and recording *The Con* quickly dissipated when they took the album on the road, though. "As much as I had creatively felt really stimulated by writing and recording the album, almost immediately the record became actually sort of a burden," Sara told *Billboard* in 2017, reflecting on the album's tenth anniversary.[50] After *The Con*'s release, Sara and Storey broke up, which not only drastically affected Sara's life, but the band's as well; Storey had been a constant presence on tours. Tegan remembers Storey training a new merch person to take over for her early in *The Con* touring cycle and afterward, when they all parted ways, everyone "just bawling in the airport." Sara also says that losing her "north star"—Storey was so comfortable with her sexuality and had helped Sara to understand hers better—contributed to what felt like a regression in dating and discussing her queerness.

"I was profoundly depressed," admits Sara, who was down to a heartsick 97 pounds then. "I hesitate to say I was suicidal, but I was thinking horrible thoughts." Tegan understood her sister's pain, but also just recalls that European tour as a miserable time. Certain gigs were "complete shit," there were multiple bus accidents, and the harsh winter weather reflected the heaviness that followed them from show to show. "She just wasn't really fun," Tegan explains, noting Sara's general demeanour during those weeks. "Things that would normally roll off her just didn't. She was just angry. Everything was a fight." That included Sara's attitude toward the press, which turned from distanced outrage to personal confrontation.

Between *So Jealous* and *The Con*, Sara says the stresses of the press and its weaponization of their sexuality or gender became crushing. For her, the press wasn't a simple stamp of approval—it represented a sector of gatekeeping that she and Tegan just couldn't break through. Though waning nowadays, its effects had a strong influence on big opportunities at the time. Sara felt the press had effectively helped blackball them from certain festival slots or TV appearances. A bad, not to mention discriminatory, review could have meant missing an opportunity to perform on Jools Holland or getting higher billing at Coachella (even though reviews aren't the only factor programmers consider). But by then, it didn't matter to Sara. It didn't matter that, again, most reviews erred positive or that journalism was shifting to let in more women, in particular at outlets like *Stereogum*, *PopMatters*, *A.V. Club*, and *Entertainment Weekly*, all of whom praised *The Con*'s complexities and the band's musical progression. Those anxieties around a few select words or a couple of derogatory lines had burrowed so deep into Sara's psyche that she believed an intervention was needed. "For me, it was about injustice," Sara asserts. "That [critics have] all this power to affect whether we get included as an important cultural touchstone, and I felt like we were getting punished because some hipster indie guys didn't like our band."

This wave of diversifying newsrooms and mastheads, which felt like it was rising in the early 2010s, was a thrilling development. It was especially encouraging for aspiring writers at the time—like me—but it also wasn't without its hardships for those who were trying to break in. My first decade of music writing consisted of working for male editors, and as someone who primarily focused on indie-rock music at first, I occasionally spotted other women writers, but people of colour felt few and far between. Whether I was attending concerts or sitting in editorial meetings, there was always an invisible barrier I felt I couldn't penetrate, like my skills as a writer alone couldn't validate me because I stuck out in every other visible way.

Throughout the years, I've seen the harsh hand of male editors push women out of music journalism, like my best friend, Jessica. While toxic work environments weren't the sole reason she switched professions almost ten years ago, we share memories (that we can laugh over now, but that are traumatizing nonetheless) of crying over men scolding us for our writing. Some of those editors were admittedly helpful in my development as a writer, but nothing compared to the lift I got when I eventually discovered entire communities of women in music journalism, and the way we helped one another with advice, sharing contacts, and providing general words of encouragement. Andrea Warner, my friend and one of the women I found early on, once told me, "By our very insistence on showing up and taking space, we are making [a space] that's a little more inclusive and reflective of the real world. Just like any other patriarchal system, you have to show up and disrupt it and sort of get in there from the inside, and hopefully it is made something fresh and new."

———————

Instead of letting publications get away with their problematic writing, as Tegan and Sara had for almost a decade, Sara decided to fight back. Frustrated by the categorization of their band as "tampon rock" in *The Con*'s *Pitchfork* review (the full line read: "Tegan and Sara should no longer be mistaken for tampon rock, a comparison only fair because of the company they kept"),[51] among other superfluous jabs, Sara reached out to *Pitchfork* via their publicist to call them out. Ultimately, only one change was made to the piece: *Pitch-fork* removed a line in the original review that referred to Walla's main occupation as being in "fellow lesbian band Death Cab for Cutie," even though the writer later noted it as a joke. "That's basically saying that being in a lesbian band is a bad thing and now you're making fun of Death Cab for Cutie using my sexuality and my lower status in your mind to put this band in a lower slot," Sara explains.

Sara laughs at it now, but remembers thinking, "Oh great, so I went to bat for the straight white guys? Don't worry, our shitty review is still there." But she wasn't alone in calling out these types of reviews. Music critic Jessica Hopper notably blogged her response to *Pitch-fork*'s "tampon rock" line: "The company they kept? Vaginas? Cos their (sic) lesbians? Is it a joke and ps. who is tampon rocking? Is that post-Lilith fair? Or just music by people who get their periods? ?!?!?!?"[52] There were similar reactions to other reviews, too, like *NME*'s two-star review that ends with the unnecessarily harsh line, "A saddening case of brick production, paper soul— here the Quins are little more than twin airbags."[53]

Over at *Rolling Stone*, critic Robert Christgau— whom other writers have defended to me as a champion of women in music—falters with the opening line of his album review: "As lesbians who never reference their oppression or even their sexuality, Tegan and Sara don't have men to lash out at, put up with, or gripe about." Christgau argues that the "objects of their romantic ambivalence remain distant"[54] and that

The Con as an album is difficult to connect with. This comes off as a form of othering by inferring that queer artists must draw from their struggles, but also that their sexuality renders them unrelatable to people like him, a straight man. "It's not written for the benefit of a male gaze, and it's not written from the perspective of a male gaze," Liss asserts, in the album's defense. "When you're a queer woman, there can be a certain kind of bro-ing down that happens with dudes, and I think the fact that *The Con* evades this is I'm sure frustrating for someone who is embedded in a certain way of thinking, let's say." It's an argument that dates back to Tegan and Sara's earliest music, that their writing sets off an alarm to readers: if you're not a lesbian, you might not get much from listening to the album. The fact that the album opens with a political statement about Sara's sexuality also seems to have escaped Christgau's critical lens. Yet another reason it's important for publications to work with diverse writers: it can prevent the kinds of glaring errors some of Tegan and Sara's most devoted fans still use to illustrate just how mistreated and misunderstood the Quins' music was.

Sara's argumentative attitude toward the press was just another way in which Sara and Tegan diverged in their approach around that time. When it came to pushing back against offensive reviews, "there was no one who was supporting me, a lot of times not even Tegan," says Sara. For Sara, this was a fight for survival, a battle not only for herself but for other marginalized acts who were being unfairly written about in ways Sara saw as damaging; these reviews can discourage other musicians, especially LGBTQ+ ones, from entering the industry. Sara continues: "I just remember having these arguments and conversations where I would be in full tears, like bawling, being like, 'Why can they talk like that about us? Why can they say those words? Why are they allowed to do this?'"

To Sara's credit, Tegan confessed that she wasn't very supportive. "I don't think I felt what she felt," Tegan explains. "I think our *Pitchfork* review was fine." It's not that Tegan was excusing the things that have been written about their band—she of course also saw the sexism behind the phrase "tampon rock"—but the bigger picture mattered more to her. Their band was selling out huge venues; "Back In Your Head" was picking up steam on the radio; *The Con* became the first Tegan and Sara album to break onto the *Billboard* chart, debuting at number 24 on the Top 200; they were making more money than they'd ever made, and Dutch DJ Tiësto (regarded by many as the "Godfather of EDM") wanted to remix "Back in Your Head." "I'm negative, too," Tegan assures. "But I'm also the kind of person who will immediately reframe something so it doesn't feel punishing. I make it useful. I use it as a way to survive these things."

Tegan's positives are worth shining a light on, especially the sold-out shows and the overwhelming support they received from fans, including a teenage me who absorbed *The Con* for months, studying every last detail of each track and memorizing lines from the accompanying DVD. It was that DVD, which I literally wore out with multiple viewings, that truly converted me from a casual fan into an obsessive. It remains a personal theory of mine that I am most drawn to musical acts that promote ideas of family and community because I spent much of high school feeling alone and desperate to find like-minded music nerds. While I eventually connected with other fans, I formed my deepest attachments to the bands themselves. But I'm not alone—other fans-turned-writers share a similar love for this album. James Rettig wrote for *One Week// One Band*: "It's probably the album that means the most to me on a personal level, the one that's shaped who I am more than any other collection of music."[55] And CBC Arts' Peter Knegt mused, "Tegan and Sara obviously are so many things to so many people, but a part of the appeal for me personally was the uncommonly detailed drama."[56]

The tensions between Tegan and Sara came to a head in Scotland during a February 2008 stop on their *The Con* tour. Just before that night's show, their tour manager asked them to reschedule a few phoners. Exhausted, Tegan and Sara turned to each other and at the same time said, "You do it." Tegan went off: "I was like, 'Fuck you, you're such an asshole, this was your interview, you need to reschedule it." Sara fought back, asking for "some fucking empathy" because she was sad. "I'm tired of you being sad!" Tegan yelled back. As Tegan walked off to rustle through her suitcase, Sara ran at Tegan and punched her in the face. Their tour manager and production manager had to pull them apart. "We were just hysterical," Tegan says. Eventually, they were talked into going onstage and performing. The crowd at that point was wild and drunk, having waited for the band to start, even after chanting their names in anticipation. As soon as the show ended, their production manager took to his Blackberry and typed up an email to them: *Take some time off, but don't quit.*

Their summer festival appearances were cancelled. Tegan attended the Juno Awards gala dinner—where they were nominated for alternative album of the year—alone because Sara refused to show up. They took some much-needed time off, apart from one another. "If I had to go back into a time machine and look at all that, and tell you what happened, I think we really just had taken on too much with the state of mind that Sara was in," Tegan concludes. The non-stop touring, the arduous schedules, all compacted by an overwhelming sense of grief, led to a moment that may have been the closest Tegan and Sara have ever been to breaking up. But as Sara told *Buzzfeed* in 2016, the gap between the end of *The Con* and the recording of their next album, 2009's *Sainthood*, forced her to realize that her "relationship with Tegan as a sister was far more important than the one in a band."[57]

Instead of sitting down and confronting the problems rooted in their conflict, the sisters did what they did best: they wrote songs. "We had chosen to just jump back into it and I think Sara and I had to get on the same page really quickly," Tegan recalls. "It felt like a reset." Sessions kicked off in New Orleans in 2008, where the two met up with the goal of doing something they had never done before: co-writing songs. In a 2009 interview with *Under the Radar*, Tegan said that Sara reached out to her after watching the 2007 Tom Petty documentary *Runnin' Down a Dream*: "Everybody writes together! Everybody from that era wrote together. We should write together." Tegan's response: "We are not Tom Petty!"[58] Up until that point, penning tracks together was an approach they hadn't explored— not just with each other, but with anyone at all. Writing was a solitary act for them both, accomplished in their own time and space, to be shared later for input and notes. That's how they'd worked since they first started to write as teenagers, and they'd continued that way as they drifted off to separate cities across the country.

In short, that co-writing sojourn wasn't very fruitful; both Tegan and Sara look back at that experiment as boring. Sitting together in a room as each worked on parts exposed the differences in their methodology more than anything. "Tegan starts with lyrics and guitar chords, whereas I like to begin with rhythm and instrumentation," Sara explained to *The Sheaf* in 2010. "I also found that I worked slowly and more meticulously. Tegan often writes quickly and impulsively."[59] Their approaches, they both realized, were the complete opposite.

Though none of the tracks they worked on in New Orleans would go with them into the studio, where they reunited with Walla, the trip wasn't a total failure. They left with two important takeaways. First, Tegan and Sara rekindled their collaborative relationship, and there was a mutual desire to continue songwriting together in some capacity. Second, the sessions inspired the themes and album title of their next release. The name of Tegan and Sara's sixth studio album, *Sainthood*, is taken from Leonard Cohen's 1979 song, "Came So Far for Beauty." During those New Orleans sessions, Sara listened to that track on repeat. She poured herself into Cohen's words, which chronicled the sacrifice and undying devotion that ultimately never yields the reward one seeks, whether that's beauty, love, or art. In the end, they chopped the song from the tracklist because they couldn't secure the rights to Cohen's lyrics, which they'd borrowed verbatim.

"I liked the idea of practising sainthood, practising being good," Sara told *Q* in 2009. "I think Tegan and I are really devoted people and we're really well behaved. We have strong romantic ideas about the future and what love should look like and what it should feel like."[60] In another 2009 interview with *Exclaim!*, Tegan said: "We think of saints as moral, devoted servants to their faith. And in love, I suppose so am I. In a much more secular, romantic way, of course."[61] For Sara, these pursuits of love extended beyond her own closest relationships—with her mother, who had by then ended her second long-term partnership, and with her grandparents, who had spent more than sixty years together—for greater insight.

The Quins did achieve one collaborative victory: "Paperback Head." It started off as a track Tegan compiled while fumbling around with Reason, an audio software. The initial result was, as she once told fans at a 2009 concert in Sweden, "a dance hit from the '90s, like something you would've heard on Club Euro '96."[62] Unsure what to do with the mash-up of sequencers, Tegan sent it to Sara, who then hopped in and wrote lyrics. Sara says the song became a formless, stream-of-consciousness experiment that Tegan didn't understand at first, but Sara fought hard to maintain.

Wanting to experiment more with techno music, Tegan was excited about the potential of "Paperback Head," but was forced to overhaul the sound when no one in the studio knew how to efficiently recreate it live. Walla's plan for *Sainthood* was to record everything live on the floor as a band, and so the final version is not a dance anthem, but something much stranger: distorted guitars punching up against a bellowing bass line, all knocking together in a jagged rhythm—it takes a moment to find your bearings when you first hear it. While the guitar riff that buzzes on the Madonna-referencing chorus feels like it was taken directly out of Tegan's repertoire, the off-kilter nature of the track often leaves fans assuming the composition is entirely Sara's. It's an odd push-pull between their respective styles, but that friction sparks a feeling of true symbiosis: proof that Tegan and Sara can create together more intensively, even if the result is received divisively by both critics and audiences. Some fans liked the sound but found Sara's lyrics indecipherable; critics like BBC's Andrzej Lukowski found it "distinctly forgettable."[63] That review included a warning that the track was actually "a testament to the fact that there really isn't much new to say about the pair's approach to *Sainthood*," suggesting Tegan's songwriting has been weighing down "the truly talented Quin." While fans love analyzing which sister wrote which songs on each album, mostly as one of many attempts to distill the differences between the two, Tegan and Sara are rarely pitted against one another as they were in that one review.

"Paperback Head" wasn't Tegan's only collaboration on the album. Three of the tracks—"Don't Rush," "Hell," "The Cure"—were co-written with AFI's Hunter Burgan, and were originally meant for a side project the two had started but failed to launch due to scheduling issues. In a 2009 *Mammoth Press* interview, Burgan, who didn't actually play on *Sainthood*, revealed that "when they went to sort out the songs they were going to record for their album, Tegan brought up some of the ones that we did and I guess everybody else really liked them."[64]

That trio of songs, which anchor the first half of the album, assert a more punk-rock direction driven by bold riffs, stomping rhythms, and some accentuating synth flourishes. "Don't Rush" and "Hell" go fast and hard; in them, Tegan revisits a performance style she has perfected over the years, revving up verses to pack in mouthfuls of lyrics. "No, I'm not ready for a big bad step in their direction/ No, I'm not ready for downtown trash, avoid collection"—she starts off "Hell" at a gradual, measured pace before hitting the gas pedal on the following lines: "Four blocks, run and hide, don't walk alone at night/ Cityscape, city change before they die/

Four blocks, I should mention in a song if I wanna/ Get along with change/ Who doesn't want to change this?" The song is equal parts about Tegan's then-Vancouver neighbourhood, which was deemed by a local paper as one of "Vancouver's four blocks of hell,"[65] and a metaphor for unrequited feelings.

The songs, which feel tight and breezy—together, thirteen tracks that come in at just under thirty-seven minutes—benefited from Walla's live band set-up, but he now sees how his plan of attack failed parts of the record, most notably some of Sara's songs. "Sara was just getting so much more into pop music," Walla notes. For Sara, songs like Robyn's "With Every Heartbeat," Alicia Keys' "Try Sleeping With a Broken Heart," and Rihanna's "Umbrella," pop songs with distinct R&B influences, became musical obsessions. Sara studied those hits like a scholar and was preoccupied with "unlocking whatever magic was happening in them," as she explained to me. This led to a more brazen embrace of the pop label, partially because she knew it would annoy the indie-rock purists around her. And as much as Sara has battled the urge to fit in in the past, she now finds even more pleasure in pushing people's buttons, challenging them to question why they hold to such rigid ways of thinking about genre, when the boundaries separating rock from pop from hip hop and more have practically dissolved in today's musical landscape.

This pop fascination was reflected in the type of songs Sara brought to the table for *The Con*, but even more so on *Sainthood*. Leaning more into synths and keyboards and moving further away from guitar-driven rock songs, Sara's side of *Sainthood* was more angular, more adventurous and etched another potential path forward for Tegan and Sara. "I feel like I gave up the guitar as a way of saying I don't want to be judged for my guitar playing anymore," Sara says, reflecting on her instrumental change-up. "I feel like, as a girl, you have to be the sickest guitar player or it's this weak spot that people will pick at. I felt so irritated all the time, and I know so many guys who play adequately, but people will go, 'Oh yeah, he's a good guitar player.'"

Sara was also single for the first time in years, which likely fanned her obsessive tendencies when it came to the pop culture she consumed, like specific documentaries or pop songs. Rediscovering the feeling of having a brand-new crush inspired her songwriting. *Sainthood*'s sequencing tells a clear story on Sara's half of the album. The opener "Arrow" finds Sara setting her sights on someone, and as the courtship unfolds over her tracks— including "On Directing" and "Red Belt"—she struggles to find a balance with this person, realizing she's fixated on every move one moment, and then is too busy to call the next. It appears that Sara is at the end of her rope until the penultimate track, "Sentimental Tune," where she musters up the courage to give it one last shot.

Her more intricate, non-traditional rock songs weren't conducive to the band arrangement, and Walla remembers Sara being freaked out about this. "There was sort of no way to get in and just rehearse them," he says, of navigating Sara's tracks. "I wish in hindsight that

I'd approached some of the album a little bit differently. It's almost like I just didn't listen to what Sara was saying. She was like, 'This isn't working for my songs,' but I was like, 'Yeah, but let's keep trying,' rather than offering alternative ways that might have worked better. I was so committed to the band-in-a-room concept." To Walla's credit, Sara said she enjoyed the challenge of recording live off the floor but agreed that the restrictions clashed with her songwriting. "Chris is right," she said. "If we had been able to be more experimental and be more into overdubbing or whatever, I feel like my songs might have felt and looked different. He didn't let my songs be as experimental as they probably could have been."

Tegan and Sara now have somewhat opposing feelings toward their songs from *Sainthood*. Both maintain that the album and the experience around making it were mostly positive, and Sara finds herself continually returning to her songs, still finding joy in playing them. But Tegan feels her side of the record is a patchwork of songs; she's less emotionally attached to them in the years since the album's release. She praises Sara's work on the album, but nitpicks her own contributions, dismissing the punky "Northshore" as random and waving off album closer "Someday" as "a weird throwback to, like, *Under Feet Like Ours*." (For the record, "Someday" is a top-notch entry in the Tegan and Sara album closer hall of fame; it ends on a syrupy note of hope where Tegan shouts mightily into the void: "Might do something I'd be proud of someday/ Mark my words, I might be something someday.")

While Tegan and Sara's songwriting and sonic styles have always been fairly distinct from one another, *Sainthood* marked a perceptible "creative divergence," according to Walla. One reason was the removal of the early writing process in which the sisters sent music back and forth to each other, fortifying ideas and challenging each other to develop songs further. "Our writing never grew," Tegan observes. "It wasn't like, oh, we've got the top-level batch where everything that's really good floated to the top. We just wrote a bunch of songs and then went into rehearsal, and we made the record out of that. It felt less like Tegan and Sara, and more like Tegan *and* Sara—separate things."

Perceptive fans felt that disconnect, too, and it turns out they're just as divided on the album as Tegan and Sara are. Some believe it's one of the band's least successful records for many of the aforementioned reasons. Some feel like *Sainthood* covers too much of the same emotional ground as *The Con*. But there are avid supporters, too, who applaud the sisters' efforts to experiment with their process. I fall somewhere in between. When I first revisited the album for this project, the high-octane energy of the songs gave me a rush similar to my first discovery of 2002's *If It Was You*. Songs like "On Directing" and the buoyantly versatile "Alligator" show the level of growth and confidence the duo gained from *The Con*. But the parts don't necessarily add up to a perfect sum, and the pleasure of feeling an entire Tegan and Sara record click into place is missing here. In the larger context of Tegan and Sara's career, it makes sense that *Sainthood* is an example of growing pains. It was an album with which they tried to forge ahead; instead, they hit a fork in the road. But without *Sainthood*, it's unclear if the rest of Tegan and Sara's career would have unfolded as it has—that's the thing about forks in the road.

Surprisingly, most critics didn't seem to mind the spasmodic sounds of *Sainthood*, which confounded Sara, who still wasn't entirely ready to let her guard down when it came to the press. "I thought people were going to focus on how weird this album was," she says. "They were going to see that Tegan wants to be in a punk-rock band and I want to be in like, an 808-sampling band or whatever. No one would get it, but then everyone liked it." *Sainthood* received its first acutely positive review from *Pitchfork*—it scored a 7.3—but also favourable write-ups from *Alternative Press*, *Spin Magazine*, *Paste Magazine*, and *Rolling Stone*. "Grown-up is a good look for the sisters, who write about romantic obsession much more compellingly than the majority of their peers," wrote *Spin*. "The tougher textures here lend weight to their descriptions of searching and not finding (or of searching and finding, and then wondering if the search was really worth all the trouble)."[66] The album went on to earn Tegan and Sara their first shortlist nomination for the Polaris Music Prize, a jury-voted annual award that crowns the best Canadian album of the year based on artistic merit. Commercially, it became the third Tegan and Sara album in a row to receive a gold certification in Canada (Music Canada's certification level changed in 2008, shifting the number of sales from 50,000 to 40,000 units sold to achieve gold), and debuted at number 21 on the US Billboard 200.

Around this time, Sara began noticing a sea change in music journalism: the slow trickle of marginalized critics entering the field was finally instigating a real shift in the way Tegan and Sara's music was analyzed and taken more seriously while leaning away from the crutch of discriminatory language. "A lot of kids who were, like, teenagers, who had grown up listening to us, were now writing about music for those same music blogs and music sites," Sara points out. "And they were being fairer. I started to finally see balance and the perspectives of writers who weren't coming at music writing with the same lens as an older male writer, and I remember being relieved—like, thank God there's a whole new generation of people who are giving us an opportunity to be reviewed without that weird baggage from the '90s and early '00s."

Being from the generation Sara speaks of, I also witnessed this recalibration of the language and vocabulary used in music first-hand. The fast-paced environment of print journalism gradually slowed down in the age of the internet, allowing for more thoughtful writing and the rise of longform reviews, features, and think pieces that could dig deeper into the art. Whether through LiveJournal entries, customized blogs, or directly on tastemaking sites, it was clear that a new wave of critics-in-the-making were eager to fight back against long-established canons that often skewed straight, white, and male. These voices would combat biases around genres like emo and pop, attempt to amend the treatment and stereotyping of women, and broaden the spectrum of LGBTQ+ and racialized perspectives, slowly creating a space in music for artists who had been on the fringe for decades. "I'd doubted whether or not it was even possible for me," Pelly says of the profession she wanted to pursue as someone who was embedded in the punk and emo scenes. "I'm so grateful to artists like Tegan and Sara whose music just made me feel like it was worth trying, at least."

Pelly, who was a few years into her career as a music journalist by 2009, says she noticed a particular effort around that time to preserve feminist voices in the music and journalism spaces, pointing to New York University's acquisition of the Riot Grrrl Collection in 2009 and the release of *Out of the Vinyl Deeps*, a collection of writing by '60s music critic Ellen Willis, as examples. This resurgence of interest in feminism and music intersected with the internet, which helped Tegan and Sara tap into and connect with their queer audience and also formed spaces for women music writers to find each other. A few years before I went to check out that Riot Grrrl collection at NYU during one of my first solo trips to New York, I attended a meet-up of women music writers thanks to a Yahoo group I'd joined. As nervous as I was leading up to that meeting at a Manhattan coffee shop—fuelled by my intense social anxiety—I felt at home almost immediately watching the women enter one by one. I didn't have to prove anything to anyone there; it didn't matter who had more experience or bigger bylines, something that men always wanted to discuss, to compare and flex. In that space, I felt that we were all equals and peers.

For a journalist like Sarah Liss, who remembers a time when no one was called out for harmful writing because "everyone just wrote homophobic and sexist things because that was just the voice," the change in dynamics and vocabulary was welcome. "I think that's affected the way people write about Tegan and Sara," she says. "You don't have people who are glomming onto those aspects of their identity as novelties anymore."

Though, of course, that kind of discourse didn't completely disappear. Being a writer with an agenda can also lead to being boxed in—like the time I was the only woman on a team of writers and was, of course, the one assigned a piece about feminism. It's a double-edged sword that elicits complicated feelings from marginalized people; we want to write about these topics but not *just* about them. Andrea Warner sums up these changes the best: "Music journalism used to be just, like, three dicks angrily hitting each other. Now, it's just two dicks angrily hitting each other—and that's progress."

For Tegan and Sara, personal change was also on the way. While touring *Sainthood*, Tegan admitted that, unlike *The Con* tour, she was the one who felt miserable. While she was proud of the record they'd put out, she'd reached a realization that their band had plateaued. It's a feeling both Tegan and Sara have faced throughout their career: a level of success unlocks, but they don't want to become complacent. Tegan started thinking, "I'm tired of being indie-rock." This was a feeling Sara had also made abundantly clear with her work on *Sainthood*: "I'm tired of playing the same rooms. What are we going to do? How are we going to grow?"

"My mood really shifts in our career when I find people get comfortable. It bothers me," Tegan continues. "I don't like patting ourselves on the back. I don't like it when, as a team, we'll reference 'Where Does the Good Go' getting on *Grey's Anatomy* or the success of 'Walking with a Ghost.' I'm like, that was years ago! I want to be uncomfortable again."

PART 4:
HIGHER PURPOSE

"BOYS OF YOUR GENERATION": This is what Rob Cavallo, then chairman of Warner Records, wrote down during a four-hour meeting with Tegan and Sara to discuss their goals and vision for their seventh album, *Heartthrob*. In reality, what Tegan had said was that she and Sara were the "voice of our generation."

It's a funny mistake, but one that got Tegan and Sara thinking. "We've always felt like reluctant, shameful sex symbols in the queer community because there's something so reductive about being a woman and being a sex symbol," Sara explains. "But there was something particularly marginalizing about being a queer sex symbol."

This line of thinking helped Tegan and Sara realize a more ambitious goal. To be seen as a queer sex symbol narrows the scope of how far an artist can make it with their music—at least that's the way LGBTQ+ artists have always been made to feel. In a 2017 interview with *PrideSource*, Amy Ray of Indigo Girls reflected on her experience being out publicly in the early '90s, noting that, "When we first came out, we were fearful of what it meant. Our biggest fear was alienating part of our audience—I wouldn't even think about that now, honestly. It's a more positive thing now. Back then it was...there was so much derogatory language around us being gay in the first half of our career. So many reviews would refer to us in a really negative way, and people would make fun of our audience. We were always the punching bag for gay humour."[67] That stigma still exists today, with an artist like Lil Nas X revealing that he was scared to come out at the age of twenty because, as a Black rapper, he wasn't sure if he'd be accepted by his peers; he told *Out* in 2021, "I don't feel like they're going to love me like that."[68]

That said, in the last twenty years or so, mainstream music—the kind that tops charts and dominates the radio—has cultivated a queer following. Some of pop's biggest stars—like Lady Gaga, Katy Perry, Ariana Grande, and Beyoncé—are all bolstered by a dedicated following of queer fans. Of those stars, only Gaga identifies as a member of the LGBTQ+ community as a bisexual woman. Even when pop stars acknowledge their queer audiences, their actions can sometimes counteract allyship, whether it's Madonna and Britney Spears kissing at the 2003 MTV Video Music Awards, a stunt that ultimately served the male gaze (think of the first person the camera cut to: Spears' ex, Justin Timberlake), or Rita Ora facing backlash for her 2018 song, "Girls," in which she fuels the male gaze by singing about kissing girls seemingly only when she drinks red wine.

Queer fans remain diehard followers of their favourite chart-topping artists partially because "our fascination with female pop stars stems from the basic need to relate and to feel seen and understood"—Bobby Box wrote this for an *In Magazine* piece that specifically looked at gay men and their idolization of female pop stars. "The pop star struggles to be taken seriously; it's a very familiar sentiment experienced by queer people."[69] But there are almost no queer people in the mainstream, no real opportunity for a direct reflection of queer experiences, and that sounded alarm for Tegan and Sara. In an interview with *Buzzfeed*, Tegan recalls a pivotal moment in their talk with Cavallo, where she said, "I can't think of a gay woman that's on the pop charts." His response: "Well, why can't that be you?"[70]

Ambition is often frowned upon, painted as selling out. But Tegan and Sara felt no shame for being open and honest about their goals. As queer artists always viewed as outsiders, this next leap was meant to show others that it was possible to break into new realms—as indie artists, as gay women, and as musicians more than a decade into a career. That last point is an important one, as pop music often favours young artists. "I feel like they probably wouldn't have been fully satisfied if they hadn't seen how popular they could get," *If It Was You* and *So Jealous* producer John Collins points out. Glass ceilings are meant to be broken, and you can't crack them if you don't try.

One of Tegan and Sara's priorities was to find someone new to slingshot their music into the pop stratosphere. Enter Greg Kurstin, an American producer whose experience in both the indie and pop realms felt like the perfect bridge. Kurstin, himself a former member of the indie-pop group the Bird and the Bee, boasts a production history spanning from Peaches and the

Shins to Pink, Sia, and Kelly Clarkson. "It was him or no one," Tegan told *Fuse* in 2016.[71] Tegan and Sara and Kurstin clicked right away. He saw their pop potential, but also an unconventionality to their songwriting that he wanted to lean into. "I think they wanted to explore some different sounds," Kurstin told *Billboard* in 2017, "a lot of them being synth- and keyboard-related, and I'm a big synth nerd from way back, so that was more than a pleasure to accommodate. They wanted to make something cool, and it was okay if there were pop songs on the record. They weren't afraid to go there."[72] In fact, they demanded it.

"He was like a wizard," Tegan adds. And, much like *The Con* and *Sainthood* producer Chris Walla, Kurstin respected the foundational demos they presented to him. According to Sara, "He was like, 'Oh great, there's already some amazing stuff here; let's work from these,' and that was very flattering to us. Greg was like, 'What are these sounds? What did you do here? I want to fiddle in your world and look at your process, and work from there,' and I felt like that was exactly what we needed." But due to Kurstin's busy schedule—in 2013, he was responsible for thirteen records, including albums by Ellie Goulding, Katy Perry, and Sia—Tegan and Sara decided to call in Justin Meldal-Johnsen (M83, Paramore) and Mike Elizondo (Pink, Eminem) for additional production help.

As evidenced in her contributions to *Sainthood*, Sara had already drafted a blueprint for the band that followed a more synth-pop-oriented style of songwriting.

Over the years, she'd often been told that her songs, like "Alligator" or "Walking with a Ghost," had "potential."

"I didn't feel like it was an insult," Sara clarifies. "People weren't saying, 'Oh, your song sucks,' but that it had the potential to be something else—and I became really interested in the 'something else.'" In her next explorations, Sara decided to distill her songwriting down to pop basics and focus on strong hooks, clearer narratives, and all-important killer bridges—something Tegan herself admits she needed help with after multiple prospective *Heartthrob* producers declared that the sisters' songs didn't have any.

This sparked a new way for Tegan and Sara to collaborate. Unlike their New Orleans sessions for *Sainthood*, during which they forced themselves to sit in a room and manifest ideas, the duo left space on their tracks for each other to have more input in the songwriting. "We realized the addition of each other can make the [songs] better," Tegan says. "That was really insightful, but it's still ultimately about my song, my experience."

"Closer," for example, was an exercise in collaboration and constant revision. Tegan is often the faster songwriter of the two, the person who can bang out a great song and not overthink it later. But with "Closer," the opening statement and lead single off *Heartthrob*, they each worked on the chorus over and over. "By the time we'd gotten to the studio I'd rewritten the song, like, six times," Tegan said in a 2013 interview with *Under the Radar*. "I felt 'Closer' was more mellow than it needed to be, so we wound up co-writing."[73]

The result is an explosive chorus that's fuelled by something Tegan had rarely written about in the past: the pure rush of blissful romance. (As lovestruck as Tegan and Sara's discography seems, most of it looks at the wrenching dark side of love.) "I was writing about my youth," Tegan stated to *Rolling Stone* upon the track's release, "a time when we got closer by linking arms and walking down our school hallway, or talked all night on the telephone about every thought or experience we'd ever had [...] It was the anticipation of something maybe happening that was truly exciting and satisfying."[74] The bubblegum burst of a chorus feels like butterflies swirling around one's stomach that first time they touch hands or kiss someone they've been crushing on. It's one of Tegan and Sara's most perfectly executed pop songs to date, and was later included as one of *Pitchfork*'s "50 songs that define the last 50 years of LGBTQ+ pride" in 2018.[75]

Writing straight-forward pop songs was an enthralling new skill for Sara to develop. "Doing all the weird in-between, nonlinear stuff is really simple," she explains. "It's like opening up a colouring book and just fucking drawing everywhere, colouring anything you want and calling it a masterpiece. But it's actually really challenging to only give yourself defined lines and then say, that's it, you really have to stay in these lines. It's super fun and challenging. *Heartthrob* was a totally new kind of challenge for me, to think in those more traditional songwriting ways." Tegan added in the aforementioned *Under the Radar* interview: "I was really trying, at that point, not to write anything really self-deprecating or self-loathing. I went back into the depths of my memory, sort of pressed the nostalgia button, and thought about finding every romantic, incredibly repressed moment and tried to draw some very simple imagery so that people would listen and be, like, 'Oh my God, that's so romantic!'"

This led to some of their most direct and emotionally robust songwriting. Songs like "Goodbye, Goodbye" and "How Come You Don't Want Me," both Sara contributions, turn common Tegan and Sara song topics of heartbreak and rejection into even more powerful gut punches. On the latter track, Sara just poses a string of direct questions that the song's title only hints at, instead of covering up hurt feelings through metaphors. Tegan's "I Was a Fool" is the band's most candid pop ballad attempt, a pristine piano-led number that uncovered a new sonic range. And on "I'm Not Your Hero," a track that feels most akin to Tegan and Sara's past material circa *So Jealous* or *Sainthood*, Sara finally confronts her outsider status, further converging her activism with her songwriting. "I'm not their hero/ But that doesn't mean that I wasn't brave," she sings over another cathartic, surging chorus. "I never walked the party line/ Doesn't mean that I was never afraid."

Heartthrob is Tegan and Sara at their clearest and most polished, an apex that feels like the culmination of years of hard work. To many in the press, it signalled a massive shift, a grand risk that was going to reap mammoth rewards. And while Tegan and Sara themselves didn't feel like the album was as seismic of a transformation, they were content with selling that story. "After so many years of doing press and feeling so out of control of the message, we were like, if we're rigid about what the messaging is, it won't be as easy for them to manipulate it," Sara discloses. "Tegan and I were mindgaming everybody. We went in saying, 'We're going to tell the press what to say about us this time. We're going to lead the press. We're going to make the plan so bulletproof and we're going to make the launch so bulletproof that it's either going to be accepted—or it's not. And everything we said, that we floated out there, we just saw it return again and again and again, and finally it morphed into *their* idea. They've created this whole idea of what this record is—except that we actually told them what it was."

The *Heartthrob* press cycle was the first time I actually spoke to Tegan and Sara, and it was clear that they were united in their messaging. But even when their answers sound stock or rehearsed—more a result of repeatedly answering the same questions as opposed to being manipulative—they've always radiated an amiability and warmth that easily disarms almost everyone they talk to.

And even though the album's title also holds another meaning—the idea of putting people you date on pedestals and idolizing them even though, over time, the fixation fades—*Heartthrob* is also a strong statement on Tegan and Sara's placement in a cisgender, heteronormative, patriarchal world. "We are heartthrobs,"

Sara says, contrasting her earlier thoughts on being a sex symbol. She admits to feeling waves of hesitation about the topic because of the complicated balance between what she personally feels versus the expectations put on her by others. "We want to own this space where we can be attractive, and where we can cast ourselves in this role that we've been reluctant to take on."

This goes hand-in-hand with another label assigned to Tegan and Sara: queer icons. It's one that grows more unnecessary as Tegan and Sara's career continues. In a 2020 interview with *Believer Magazine*, Tegan expressed clear discomfort around the label, noting "I think of how many other queer artists weren't recognized, and I just shy away from even acknowledging our icon status. I hate it. [...] I don't want to be called that. And then I also want to be seen as that. It's complicated."[76]

Less than a year after that interview, I asked Tegan and Sara individually whether they feel like queer icons. Funny enough, their initial reactions were identical: they each Googled the meaning of "icon." (I audibly laughed as I told Tegan that Sara had done the exact same thing the day before; Tegan, focused on pulling up the definition, was unsurprised.) "A person or thing regarded as a representative symbol or as worthy of veneration," Tegan read aloud. The idea of being an icon generally brings up feelings around aging for Tegan, who actively rejects the positioning of her and Sara as veterans who are nearing the end of their career. She also adds that her hesitation around the label is grounded in the inherent shame women feel about taking up too much space.

Ultimately, though, she retracts her earlier thoughts: "I am an icon and I am a genius." Not only does she say this with pride, but as a way of reclaiming words that men of all ages have easily embraced throughout history. Sara similarly accepts the status, specifying that "at least for one generation, we are some of the most successful queer people in a certain genre. We're not fucking Beyoncé, but for a certain generation, we're like gay astronauts. We went to a new planet, and we were the first ones there. So I'll take that."

———

Heartthrob reviews were pretty unanimously positive. *Billboard* called the twins' "dazzling pop rebirth"[77] one of the year's best, a bold proclamation to make in January. *Spin Magazine* noted that "Bright, busy and unapologetically direct, *Heartthrob* nonetheless makes everything Tegan and Sara did before seem perversely obscure," but added, "the Quins never sound like anyone but themselves."[78] Even *NME*, a publication that has a history of being unfriendly toward Tegan and Sara, went above and beyond by describing *Heartthrob* as a "triumph."[79] The album landed Tegan and Sara a second Polaris Music Prize shortlist nomination (they lost to Montreal experimental rock band Godspeed You! Black Emperor's *Allelujah! Don't Bend! Ascend!*). And they finally earned their first Juno Award win after five previous nominations. *Heartthrob* took home group of the year, pop album of the year, and single of the year for "Closer."

Tegan still sees events like the Junos to be more of an "extravaganza" than an achievement, but it was this particular award show that helped her realize how much that kind of recognition meant to everyone around her and Sara, from their parents to their longtime management team. "I remember my parents' faces," she says, brushing past the stressful moments and preparation for their big performance. "It was just pure joy and pride oozing out of them. Like, my dad cried, and my dad doesn't cry. This was so validating to the people who love us and care about us and who've worked with us. I didn't realize how significant it would be for our managers, who've been working with us since 2002, to finally have their artists on that stage. That's why the Juno wins for *Heartthrob* felt so special."

"Closer" quickly became Tegan and Sara's biggest hit to date. The song topped Billboard's Hot Dance Club Songs chart; it became their first single to ever land on the Billboard Hot 100, peaking at 13; it went platinum in Canada within a year of its release; and its music video is their most popular on YouTube, with more than 23 million views. They were invited to perform on *David Letterman* and *The Ellen Show*, and the song was even covered on an episode of *Glee*, a TV series that was, at that point, reeling in approximately five million viewers each week and went on to win two GLAAD Awards.

Their music was also beginning to show up on fellow pop stars' radars. On August 3, 2013, Tegan and Sara joined Macklemore & Ryan Lewis onstage at Montreal's Osheaga Festival to perform the LGBTQ+ anthem

"Same Love." Later that month, Tegan and Sara were invited to perform "Closer" with Taylor Swift, who first discovered Tegan and Sara's music via a movie trailer for Darren Stein's film *G.B.F.*[80] Swift apparently quickly became obsessed with *Heartthrob* —so much so that, on the evening of Swift's Los Angeles show at the Staples Center, she told the 20,000 fans in attendance: "I think that this album is one of my favourites of all time. If you've ever had your heart broken, you need this album."[81]

Sara likens Swift to another legendary artist they once opened for: "Not unlike the Neil Young experience, I think that there's something about the way someone treats you that can have a long-term impact. She was extremely nice. I mean, she made us fucking biscuits and jam, and she knew our songs, and was so complimentary. And the show was just different. I always feel like I'm on *Star Search* when I do those types of arena shows, like I'm in somebody's documentary series or something. It just feels like everything is happening and all you're thinking is, 'I don't want to get my hand trapped under one of those stages that's moving really fast.'"

At the end of 2013, Tegan and Sara attended the Billboard Women in Music gala and got to pay tribute to one of the evening's honourees and an idol of theirs, Pink. (Sara got a big laugh out of the pop star, and everyone in attendance, when she announced, "I know you're not gay—yet."[82]) They notched even more arena time in 2014 when Katy Perry invited them to open her

Prismatic North American tour. This pivot back to being an opening act—during this time, they also shared the bill with Fun. and Lady Gaga—definitely felt weird at times, but it was also a good glimpse at the top-tier pop world that Tegan and Sara had aspired to break into with *Heartthrob*. "I remember feeling like, okay, this is a change of pace," Sara says. "It was kind of scary and thrilling to be in front of an audience that you have to kind of convince you're worthy of being paid attention to." With the goal to reach wider audiences, these types of opportunities were a way of winning potential new fans. For Sara, the novelty of everything *Heartthrob* granted is similar to another momentous time in their career. "*So Jealous* just blew the doors open," Sara says, looking back at their 2004 breakout release. "These two albums are so similar in my mind because of what they did for us—there was just this buzzing craziness."

But growing pains meant that some of their loyal fans felt left behind. Fans who felt extremely invested in Tegan and Sara's career made claims that they were selling out or abandoning the queer community in order to assimilate into the mainstream. And whereas Sara once struggled with press criticism, she shares that it was Tegan who felt more hurt by the judgement of their closest followers: "I really watched Tegan suffer from fan comments, and they really made her feel insecure."

Heartthrob would be the last straw for Tegan, who says she had to sever the tie between herself and her most brash, vocal fans, for her own wellbeing and mental health. Learning that the band's move into pop felt like an attack on their fans' sexualities was something Tegan couldn't understand, even as she recognized the feeling as valid: "I would never take that away from them, it's fair." Because Tegan and Sara spent their careers first inadvertently and only later actively cultivating a queer audience, their identities as community leaders and fringe outsiders were important to their most loyal following. Expanding that focus felt disappointing, even though the Quins tried to make it clear that their desire to break out wasn't about shedding their queerness as much as displaying it on a bigger platform. That's part of the reason Tegan and Sara were so vehement with their messaging around *Heartthrob*: to explain to fans why they were doing what they were doing. Tegan doesn't fault people for outgrowing their music, but the direction of their ire against her—during a time when social media was reaching its most popular and influential point—was too much.

"I cared deeply about what people thought," she says. "After *Heartthrob*, I didn't put up a wall, but I started to be like, 'Okay, that's not real.' I think there's a community of people in every band's fandom that thinks about this stuff, and I used to be tapped into what those fans thought because I liked them. I wanted them to like us, and I wanted them to feel seen and for them to know that we cared. I still really care, but I know from experience that if you went through a fucking breakup and *The Con* had just come out, that's always going to be your record. And you might hear a new record and go, 'Yeah, it's got some good gems on it; anyway, I like

King Princess now.' I'm not gonna take that personally. That's great. King Princess is awesome. I'll see you at her concert! I don't think my empathy is gone."

Conversely, Sara's take on fan reactions is surprisingly nonchalant. She takes some small pleasure from the power dynamics at play here, as opposed to the imbalance she feels with the press, who have control over what gets published and who judges their music. "When fans were like, 'Why are you doing this?' or 'Why do you sound like that?' it actually made me feel like I was doing exactly what I should be doing." While Sara felt powerless against professional critics, her feelings toward her own audience were more self-assured, even edging on hubristic. "I've fought so long and hard to do what I do that I'm not going to have you eat me alive and tell me what to do," she says defiantly, although it feels like she's unwittingly addressing both fans and critics in this moment. "If you don't like it, that's one thing, but if you come at me and try to make it seem like I've done you wrong—like, get a grip. That is not what this is about."

Even though the pushback from some fans seemed loud, many other fans were overjoyed for their success and felt a sense of pride that a band they've been shouting about for years had finally found their way in front of people otherwise oblivious to their talent. Tegan and Sara met their goal to gain new fans, and with more eyes focused on them came more opportunities to maintain a certain level of attention—which meant an even more stuffed schedule and list of responsibilities.

An average day during the *Heartthrob* years could start early in the morning with a radio appearance, followed by an early evening opening slot, capped off by one more obligation later at night. For better or worse, their pop-star ambitions also came with an overwhelming schedule of pop-star proportions. And that's when Tegan and Sara began to understand that as much as this album cycle was checking off boxes on their wish list, that level of stardom was perhaps not sustainable for them. "We were just really stretched thin," Sara acknowledges, looking back at those dizzying days. "Nothing but respect for the people who do it, but it's like being around athletes—it just requires something so different from what we have." Tegan doesn't go as far as calling some of their extra engagements a regret, but she does recognize that she and Sara transformed into "a band that said yes to a lot of stuff"—perhaps too much. "Opening for Katy Perry was really good, but did it help us sell records or help with radio? No," Tegan admits, "but I think we learned a lot from the experience."

———

One of the lessons they took away from inhabiting those spaces was how to build a larger production for their own headlining tour, which came shortly after they wrapped up their time on the road with Perry. For their 2014 Let's Make Things Physical tour in May and June, Tegan and Sara's stage bore an intricate lighting system, two risers for them each to perform on (the lighting director told the twins, "You guys are too short, no one can see you"), and, for the first time ever, they performed without instruments for parts of the show.

It was a freedom they hadn't experienced onstage. It was a divisive move, but these tweaks also meant a lot to other fans who'd been used to seeing Tegan and Sara's shows staged similarly for years—down to Tegan always being on the right side of the stage and Sara on the left. "The first time I got onstage with just a microphone, I was trembling," Sara recalls. "You have to be aware of your body all the time. There's a sort of flexing with the guitar that happens, but all of sudden I had to be so present. What I also found happening was that I could disappear easier onstage without the guitar. Like, if I wanted to be somewhere else in my mind, or if I wanted to be big, or if I wanted to be small—I could do whatever I wanted."

That freedom quickly curdled to anxiety during their bigger moments, like that 2015 Academy Award performance with the Lonely Island for "Everything is Awesome." Selected by the comedy trio to perform the film's quasi-theme song, Tegan and Sara never expected their small contribution to *The Lego Movie* soundtrack to snowball into an extra year of promotion tacked onto the two-year album cycle for *Heartthrob*.

It's not that Tegan and Sara didn't value the opportunities, or that they didn't have any fun, but these experiences hit the limits of their comfort levels. It's something Tegan acknowledges as a weakness, but not necessarily detrimental. "As a band, we don't aspire to celebrity or fame. I'm so fucking glad we got to be on the Oscars, that we got to tour with Katy Perry, that we got to play on *The Ellen Show*...those were all really important, but we're not comfortable in that world. My memory of a lot of those really big things we did was just nervousness and wanting it to be over, and then an incredible amount of guilt because I felt like I was lacking gratitude." She refuses to watch those moments—she has never seen their Oscars performance nor their big appearance onstage with Taylor Swift—because it forces a moment of reflection that's discomforting. "I'm terrified it will ruin it and the next time I'll be thinking, 'Oh God, don't do that thing you did onstage with Taylor.'"

––––––––––

Heartthrob unlocked many exciting possibilities for Tegan and Sara, but the only one they wanted to pursue with their next record, 2016's *Love You to Death*, was their new sound. Synth-pop, as well as the refreshingly direct songwriting of *Heartthrob*, became a new template, and songs continued to pour out effortlessly. "I knew we were going to stay in that lane," Tegan notes. "We could still make a pop record, but without the crushing psychological weight of knowing that we had to promote it in the same way we had with *Heartthrob*." That meant learning to say no to opportunities, and, in a move to prioritize mental health and avoid burnout (something many musicians overlook and suffer the consequences of later on), Tegan and Sara administered new guidelines to their day-to-day workload. "After *Heartthrob*, we added a line item to all of our budgets," Tegan explains, "which I call the emotion line item: if we're doing something purely for money, there had better be a lot of zeroes. If we're doing it purely to get out of debt, if we're doing it purely to fill a day or do something for our label, then we need to assign it an emotional value. Like, we didn't get paid to do the Oscars and it was really traumatizing, but the emotional value of it was huge because it was an incredible milestone for our band, and it was an incredible payoff in terms of all the work we put into it. So learning to say no, and learning to defend ourselves when it comes to these decisions, has become a huge part of our career."

As they'd observed during their previous album cycle, the pop landscape was still lacking in queer perspectives. Seedlings were sprouting, though, and in the aftermath of *Heartthrob*, artists like Troye Sivan, Hayley Kiyoko, and Kehlani began gaining more mainstream momentum. "Everyone was affected by the scene they created," according to Halifax pop artist Ria Mae, who opened for Tegan and Sara on their 2017 European tour.

"I feel like Tegan and I have made a massive effort over the last ten years to create a community that we didn't feel we had in the first ten years of our career," Sara told *Entertainment Weekly* in 2017.[83] (With only a handful of pop-cultural touch points to guide them growing up, such as k.d. Lang, Melissa Ethridge or Ani DiFranco, Tegan and Sara felt they'd lacked real-life queer mentors upon first entering the music industry.) "Some of [using our platform] is about visibility and queer people of colour and social justice. And some of it is just, 'Hey, I saw you put a record out, you're young and this industry can be crazy, here's my number, call me anytime.' [...] That stuff is really important to us personally." At a 2017 concert at London's Roundhouse, Tegan told fans, of selecting their opening acts: "We go out of our way to find alternative voices because there just isn't a lot of room for alternative voices in the mainstream."[84]

Shamir Bailey, a Las Vegas–born musician, says their constant support is not only greatly appreciated, but also deeply meaningful. "Any time they post about me or my music, it's genuinely because they keep up and they like it. That's just so crazy to me because I wouldn't be here without them. I'm not sure I would have wanted to tackle music in this way if it wasn't for them, truly."

Australian pop-rocker Alex Lahey is another artist who says she would not be where she is today without Tegan and Sara's generosity. Lahey learned to play the guitar by listening to *The Con*, and when both bands ended up performing at the Splendour in the Grass music festival in Yelgun, New South Wales, Lahey saw it as meeting her idols. "That whole 'Don't meet your heroes' thing is a lie," she says, laughing. Lahey, a rising star who earned her place at the festival by winning a local radio contest, says a piece of advice Sara imparted was particularly eye opening. She wells up with emotion as she retells the story.

"I was in a position where I was getting asked to do queer press and media and, at the time, as a young person, I was really worried that I was going to get pigeonholed," she says. She looked at Sara and asked, "You guys have forged such a path, you guys made it possible for people like me to be where I am, what do you think?"

Sara's advice to Lahey: "The reason we've been so passionate about forging a path is so that the path can continue to be forged by people like you. If you perpetuate what you think the norm should be, then the norm will follow." About the press, Sara told Lahey to tell interviewers, "Being queer is totally normal and it shouldn't be made into a big deal at all."

"I have taken that to heart," Lahey says. It's four years after that meeting and having opened for Tegan and Sara on their *Love You to Death* tour. "This advice applies to everything, and I've held that sentiment very, very, very close to me. It's been a cornerstone of my decision making in my career and in my life."

This quest for queer visibility—not just in mainstream pop—started long before Tegan and Sara and still has a long way to go, which Lahey recognizes. But this is the change Tegan and Sara have always, in some way, wanted to see happen, and now they've created the community to power that evolution. Lahey says with confidence that an integral part of the sisters' legacy is to have created a new norm.

The act of extending support to other artists takes a lot of kindness, which Bailey notes the music industry often lacks. "Sometimes it feels like a death sentence to be labelled as nice in the music industry," he explains. "But that's something I strive for. There's been plenty of times throughout my career where I kind of feel like, 'Am I being naive? Do I need to toughen up or, like, sit this out?' But to see [Tegan and Sara] still have that kind of level of care and compassion—and have the longevity that they have within the industry—definitely just gives me a bit of solace that, you know, kindness basically trumps all."

For Tegan and Sara, the space they've fought for in pop, and are now seeing populated by other up-and-coming queer acts, still feels rare. To truly use that platform they've built, they wanted to be loud, proud, and more explicitly queer than they'd ever been before in their music. Their music rarely addressed their sexual preferences or used pronouns to specify the subjects in their songs—although their queerness has always been present by virtue of them being queer women writing songs about love.

That's what makes "Boyfriend," the lead single off 2016's *Love You to Death*—an album that reunited Tegan and Sara with Greg Kurstin—such a powerful standout. The song was written by Sara about a woman (her now-partner, who had not dated a woman prior to Sara) who was reluctant to define their relationship. "I spent many years feeling bad about falling almost exclusively for women who identified as straight before they met me," Sara explained to *Lez Spread the Word* in 2018. "But then I started to reflect deeply on my gender and realized that I am probably more male-identified when it comes to romance and relationships."[85] The resulting single plays with gender roles, with Sara identifying as a boyfriend instead of a girlfriend and identifying her subject by using she/her pronouns. These details are subtle, but their impact is tremendous for queer people who don't always get to see themselves clearly defined. "You treat me like your boyfriend/ And you trust me like a, like a very best friend," Sara sings with melodic anguish on the bubbling synth-pop song. Its chorus concludes with a line that is universal, but also a feeling that resonates even more strongly for LGBTQ+ listeners who've been through similar experiences: "I don't want to be your secret anymore." *Spin Magazine*'s Rachel Brodsky praised the track for reflecting positively "on pop's growing diversity," adding, "they've simultaneously grown more famous while reaching an even greater level of comfort in the details they choose to reveal."[86]

Sara told *Beats 1* that the concept of being kept a secret by one's partner "doesn't seem immediately relatable to everybody, whether they're straight or whatever. But this idea, you know, that we've all been in that situation where we really like someone and we want to make it official and they're not ready, that's what the song is about."[87] And there were other side effects. As Sara told the *New York Times*, "This is the first time in our career where I'm getting a lot of men saying to me like, 'I totally relate to this song.' And I [was] completely surprised."[88]

Sara admits that the song puts a twist on gender, but shares that it's also the most accurate portrayal of her gender and sexuality in a song yet. Around 2009's *Saint-hood*, both Tegan and Sara began self-identifying as, and using the term, 'queer' rather than 'lesbian' or 'gay.' In the decade leading up to that change, the terms 'lesbian' and 'gay' had been used to marginalize them as artists by the media, to signal to people (largely straight men) that Tegan and Sara's music wasn't for them. Those terms became maligned, but they weren't 100 percent factual either. "We both became very uncomfortable with being called lesbian because it felt very gendered," Tegan told *Proud Radio* in 2020. "I just found myself cringing when that word was used. It felt very feminine, and as someone who has never really felt feminine, it felt like the wrong word for me. We adopted queer, and, for me, it encompassed my gender and my community. So it wasn't just about my sexuality, it's that I'm queer; I'm different, I'm alternative. I felt queer really needed to be taken back and adopted by our community." Sara added: "It's a disruptive word and when I use it, I like that it makes people uncomfortable, especially straight people."[89]

On "BWU" ("Be Without You"), another splashy '80s-inspired synth track on *Love You to Death*, Sara revisits the idea of queerness and marriage, something she explored years earlier on *The Con*'s "I Was Married." Since *The Con*'s release, the US Supreme Court has ruled same-sex marriage legal across the country, a monumental change that Sara says gave her a sense of pride and the freedom to truly express how she feels about the institution of marriage. "BWU" furthers the disdain expressed on "I Was Married," with Sara defiantly saying she doesn't need a wedding at all. (Sara has since married her new partner, though she notes in our conversations that the decision was influenced by the fact that her partner is American and marriage was a way to secure permanent resident status in Canada. Interestingly enough, Sara and I share the same views on marriage, and I have also married my partner of nine years for the same reason.)

Love You to Death is undoubtedly Tegan and Sara's most explicitly queer album, and it's also their most personal in other ways. Even though Tegan previously wrote about her relationship to Sara on the *Under Feet Like Ours* highlight "Divided," it's Sara here who digs into even darker memories, confronting times when the two drifted apart and times when that tension escalated to ugly actions, like during the tour for *The Con*.

At the heart of *Love You to Death* is a pair of songs, "White Knuckles" and "100x," both written by Sara. "My life tethered like/ like a twin or a son," she opens on the former, a booming, spacious piano ballad that builds into a dramatic chorus. "Scared to be severed right/ right before we begun/ Doubled like a couple, we stood/ Stood out in the light, light." Tegan was actually in the studio when Sara wrote "100x," an even more stripped-down piano number on which Sara admits to Tegan: "It was cruel of me to do what I did to you/ It was wrong of me to hurt such a big part of you."

"Tegan popped in while I was writing the lyrics, and it was funny because she would pipe up and say, 'What if you sing this thing? Or that thing?' And I was like, this is so awkward," Sara told *Time* while promoting this album. "I'm trying to use our experience as sisters and our conflict when we were younger. I'm not saying that in the room, but that's what I'm doing. I'm almost creating the conflict anew. I'm like, 'No, I don't really like that line.' I can see her getting frustrated, like, 'I'm just trying to help!' And I'm like, 'I know.' But it was really helpful. I was really tapping back into how complicated our relationship is."[90] That same directness they delivered on *Heartthrob* is applied equally here, with Sara's weighty, intricate feelings as bare as they've ever been. In *The Atlantic*'s review of the album, writer Spencer Kornhaber noted how well that simplicity works: "They bring a scientist's rigor and an editor's clarity to the stereotypically mushy topic of love, as well as, lately, to the synth-pop template they've helped repopularize on radio. Their trick is conveying lots of information—melodic, rhythmic, and lyrical—while maintaining simplicity and elegance."[91] Yet the versatility of their songwriting also means that these songs can be interpreted as simple breakup songs, too.

The darker, more personal themes on *Love You to Death*—a convergence of Tegan and Sara's new pop sound and the more heart-wrenching, detailed songwriting that defined their earlier work—gave the sisters' pop signature more depth. But some listeners overlooked that incremental growth, comparing it to the monumental leap on *Heartthrob*. While *Pitchfork* acknowledged Tegan and Sara as "a crucial voice in the pop landscape," they also noted: "After such an impressive and self-imposed breakaway, it's a bit of a shame that their new album, *Love You to Death*, feels like a focused retread of its predecessor."[92]

In my own first few listens of the album, I also wasn't immediately hit with that same sugar rush of melodies that *Heartthrob* gave me, but it's an album that grows with each listen. If *Heartthrob* was a gut punch, then *Love You to Death* is more of a slow build that grows addictive over time. Now, a few years removed from its release, I'm constantly surprised by how much the lyrics and rhythms have burrowed inside my brain, and how fast its 31-minute runtime goes by, prompting repeat listens over hours and days. If anything, some of the '80s influence on the tracks can feel divisive, depending on one's interest in, or tolerance of, glossy synths.

Heartthrob and *Love You to Death*—the latter of which is Tegan and Sara's last album of new, original material for the time being—signalled the musical trend of indie acts shifting toward synth-pop. *The Con* and *Sainthood* producer Chris Walla even argues that Tegan and Sara deserve full credit for pioneering that move; he claims that Tegan and Sara's successful transition was like a permission slip for everybody else.

In an essay for *Pitchfork* titled "How Indie Went Pop—and Pop Went Indie—in the 2010s," writer Jayson Greene wrote, "There was a certain anything-goes panic to the era, and that chaos had some salutary effects, one of which was that people slid across the lines between indie and mainstream so violently that there was no need to pretend to take firm sides anymore."[93]

The piece points to examples like Bon Iver's Justin Vernon teaming up with Kanye West, Vampire Weekend's Ezra Koenig scoring a songwriting credit on Beyoncé's *Lemonade*, and artists like Grimes, Sky Ferreira, and Charli XCX blurring the lines between indie and pop. But it never once names Tegan and Sara. Interestingly, as soon as Sara noticed other people taking their lead, that knee-jerk reaction to swerve away from the pack kicked in. "By the end of *Heartthrob*, I was already like, 'Oh, everybody's a pop singer. Now everybody's going to write top lines for pop singers,' and that immediately made me want to go away and do something else. I don't want to compete for sessions with other indie-rock musicians to write top lines for Sia. No thanks."

Heartthrob's influence also seeped into the sounds of prominent pop albums in the years that followed. Swift, who publicly proclaimed her love for the record, released the acclaimed *1989*, which went on to take home the Grammy award for album of the year. Swift herself was already on a pop trajectory long before Tegan and Sara came into her life, but whereas her previous album, *Red*, explored more rock and EDM-driven pop templates, *1989*—which included collaborations with *Heartthrob*'s "How Come You Don't Want Me" co-writer, Jack Antonoff—went full '80s synth-pop. Antonoff even noted the following to *Buzzfeed* in 2016, not in reference to Swift: "You would go into the studio with an artist and you'd be like, 'What are you into lately?' And they'd be like, *Heartthrob*. 'What kinda vibe do you wanna do?' *Heartthrob*."[94]

Pop artist Carly Rae Jepsen went as far as to reach out directly to Tegan and Sara to collaborate. The Canadian singer told *Time*, "I was knocking on Tegan and Sara's door myself, reaching out to artists I love and sending them personal emails: 'Hey, my name's Carly, I want to try something a little different. Want to get in a session this week?'"[95] Of course by then Jepsen was a star in her own right via the megahit "Call Me Maybe," but as someone who is also motivated to switch up her style, Jepsen's follow-up album, *Emotion*, saw her teaming up with dozens of songwriters, producers, and artists. Unfortunately, Tegan and Sara's contribution didn't make the cut—of the songs they worked on, Tegan and Sara told *Time*, "Some of them are songs that we ended up taking back in and are considering shopping around or using ourselves"[96]—but again, *Heartthrob*'s sonic influence shines through in moments on the synth-laden *Emotion*.

"It's to the point where I've heard music and gone, 'Is that the new Tegan and Sara?'" *So Jealous* and *The Con* collaborator Matt Sharp says of Tegan and Sara's impact during these outstanding years. "And it turns out it's just somebody else that's obviously heavily influenced or inspired by them." Sharp references the famous quote that's been attributed to Brian Eno over the years about how the Velvet Underground only sold 30,000 records during their first five years, but "everyone who bought one of those 30,000 copies started a band."

"I feel that way about Tegan and Sara," Sharp continues. "Not that they've sold a certain number of records; obviously they've been really successful. But their music opened people up to the fact that they could do this, too."

―――――――

For their *Love You to Death* tour, Tegan and Sara decided to donate a percentage of the proceeds to an organization. Their manager sent them a list of places to consider, but nothing corresponded with the issues that Tegan and Sara cared most about: women's and LGBTQ+ rights. A frustrated Tegan shared this in conversation at a dinner party, and the woman she was talking to made an obvious suggestion: "You should start your own foundation." That conversation put the wheels in motion. Committed to creating something that wasn't just a vanity project, Tegan and Sara dove into research. During the *Love You to Death* tour, they met with countless organizations, activists, researchers, legislators, and even fans at their shows to get a better understanding of what issues needed to be addressed within the LGBTQ+ community. Some of the people they met included members of GLAAD, the Audre Lorde Project, the LA LGBT Center, and Equality North Carolina. "We played shows every night," they later wrote in a press release, "but it was also an important listening and learning tour for us."[97]

The Tegan and Sara Foundation formally launched in December 2016. That timing proved even more serendipitous given that year's US election, in which Republican candidate Donald Trump beat out democratic nominee Hilary Clinton to become the 45th president. The day before the election, Tegan and Sara were invited to perform at NPR's famed Tiny Desk Concert, a performance series set in the public broadcaster's office space in Washington, DC. During that session, Sara told the small audience: "We're going to be here tomorrow. We're going to watch history be made."

The following day, the band enjoyed a day off in Washington. Tegan now admits that she "felt so sure that [Clinton] wasn't going to win." Perhaps it was the conversations she and Sara had had with various activists and nonprofit organizations, where people expressed both anxiety about Trump's potential win and preparedness. "None of them were surprised," Tegan says. Almost everyone they'd spoken to had prepared lists of acts that might be enacted or attacked and rights that might get rolled back. It was as if the organizers were bracing for combat, and both sisters sensed that ominous energy in the air. It didn't make the moment of Trump's win any less "fucking depressing," according to Tegan. Her memory of election day is still burned into her brain: they went sightseeing and later purchased a spread of food and drinks for a viewing party in their hotel room. "It's funny in hindsight," Tegan continues, "just how low energy we were that day. It was clear. We knew."

The mission statement for the Tegan and Sara Foundation is simple: to improve the lives of LGBTQ+ women and girls. "I think that one of our lasting impressions of our tour is there is a hopefulness," Sara said in an early video filmed to promote their foundation. In that same video, Sara added, "We will fight against the repressive legislation of the incoming Trump administration."[98] Together, they pledged, we can make a difference.

That meant supporting and directing funds to other established causes like the Audre Lorde Project, Eagle Canada, the Astraea Lesbian Foundation for Justice, Out on Screen, and the Zebra Coalition, the last of which is an organization that provides services for LGBTQ+ youth (ages thirteen to twenty-four) that Tegan and Sara have backed for years through donations from their merch sales. The Tegan and Sara Foundation took that partnership one step further by funding six months of transportation for youth to access school, employment, and medical and mental health counselling appointments.

The foundation has also created some of its own programs, such as QueerHealthAccess.com, a resource launched in September 2017 to help people locate LGBTQ-competent healthcare. And that programming continues to expand to include community grants and funding for LGBTQ+ summer camps. "When I think about being a queer teenager and getting to actually meet other queer teenagers it kind of blows my mind, so we really want to get involved in helping grow some of the existing camps that exist in North America that are very underfunded," Sara told *Las Vegas Weekly* in 2017.[99]

"The Foundation just honestly feels like a concretized version of what they've been doing this whole time," according to artist and director on the Tegan and

Sara Foundation board Vivek Shraya. Shraya adds that starting this organization is an impressive feat for the Quins, who already have a lot of work on their plates to begin with ("This is like a second job on top of multiple other things"). The foundation's board members also include the Obama Foundation's Aditi Hardikar, Muslims for Progressive Values ambassador Blair Imani, actor and activist Elliot Page (who name-checked Tegan and Sara during a speech in 2014 announcing he was gay), and Emy Storey.

The foundation was met with overwhelmingly positive feedback, but the process of getting funding was harder than Tegan and Sara had anticipated. Tegan says that they probably hit the ground too hard with a "naive enthusiasm," and while fans at shows were more than happy to help—Tegan and Sara shows now often have two set-ups: a merch table alongside a designated table where fans can go and learn more about the foundation, pick up some free postcards, or donate directly—bigger corporations were tougher to win over. "I just thought, 'Well, we'll probably get hundreds of thousands of dollars every year from big organizations who want to support gay people, like the people who pay Katy Perry to play Pride, right?" Tegan muses. "No, that's not how it works."

The Quins' status as cis white women put them in a position of privilege over others, something Sara realized early on and articulated in an introductory video about the foundation: "We recognize that we can't just sort of jump in and solve every issue or solve every problem." Tegan concurs: "We think of ourselves as DIY...but the reality is that we benefit from the system that we're a part of. We're part of the major label system. We're part of a major publisher system. And we're white, so we went in with this, 'We're going to help you marginalized people, blah blah blah,' not realizing that, yes, we're marginalized-ish but within that community, no, we're not." When certain parts of the world were hit with the COVID-19 pandemic in early March 2020, coinciding with continuing protests around anti-Black racism and violence, Tegan and Sara made sure the foundation directed grants to Black-led, LGBTQ+ organizations addressing systemic racism by organizing an end to police violence and providing legal counsel, policy development, and mental health services.

In 2018, Tegan and Sara were the recipients of a National Arts Centre Award and honoured as musicians, songwriters, and activists. Their speech at the 2018 Governor General's Performing Arts Awards focused on the reason they continue to fight for LBGTQ+ youth and representation: "Our queer identity and our activism have been the thread that has stitched our personal lives and our professional lives together," Sara said with sincere gratitude. "For both of us, the greatest gift of this life and career has been the opportunity to redistribute our time, energy, and money back into the community that we belong to and that we care so deeply for." Tegan added: "As mentors, role models, and now activists, Sara and I have found an even higher purpose for our lives."[100]

CONCLUSION

By the time you read this, Tegan and Sara have likely released a handful of new projects. When the COVID-19 pandemic pressed pause on the entire world in early 2020, many people—myself included—were frozen with fear and anxiety. The idea of finishing this book felt like an impossible feat. For starters, I was supposed to board a plane that summer to Vancouver to spend time in person with Tegan and Sara. For the entire month of April, I would wake up every day uncertain of how to move forward with this project, capsized and drowning in self-doubt. In many ways, it was actually the ideal time to revisit Tegan and Sara's music, to draw comfort from nostalgic tunes—something a lot of people did in order to cope with the mounting tension threatening to crush us all—but also to use it as a fitting soundtrack for my distressed feelings.

By the time I actually scheduled my first calls with Tegan and Sara in late April—over the phone, before I could sort out how to use the now-essential video service Zoom—the Quin sisters, who were both quarantining on Canada's west coast, had already hit the ground running on various projects that didn't require them to be on the road. Over the months, as I periodically caught up with them, they would reveal the slew of new hobbies and professional ventures they were each working on. One day, Sara would be gardening. Another day,

Tegan would talk about the graphic novel series she and Sara were writing. While music continues to be Tegan and Sara's main medium, publishing their debut book *High School* sparked a different love of writing that was challenging and, at times, conjured a sense of fear that Sara felt particularly energized by: "I'm aware I always have the safety net of knowing that I can perform and I can always make music. I'm not afraid now of waking up and not knowing how to do that."

As the months rolled by, they added another book to their slate—a follow-up to *High School* that's about the science and psychology behind twins. And that's just beginning of a long list of projects: an audio project that will accompany their new book; a TV adaptation of *High School* that was picked up by IMDb TV; pivoting the Tegan and Sara Foundation to address COVID-19-related issues; a remix EP of songs from *Hey, I'm Just Like You*; an album of reworked songs from their teenage years that accompanied *High School*; plus, musical collaborations with Beach Bunny and Pom Pom Squad. Tegan became a board member of the Foundation Assisting Canadian Talent on Recordings (FACTOR) to better help enact change from inside the music industry. And somewhere in it all, they also began writing a new album. Individually, Tegan adopted a dog and Sara moved into a new home. All this while I could barely get out of bed.

For a band that's been around for more than two decades now, it feels like Tegan and Sara have more energy than ever before. This isn't to say that they, like all other artists during the pandemic, didn't have their own concerns over the future of the music industry, but Tegan and Sara are perhaps at their most creative and motivated in times of change. (Of course, they also have the privilege of being successful—something they both acknowledge.) Much like their early albums, the first handful of years in Tegan and Sara's career felt bogged down by various things: a hesitation to foreground their queerness; a constantly evolving sound that they couldn't fully call their own; a press machine that was at times relentlessly cruel. It took the sisters a number of years to break free and crack the code to a career where they were unafraid to pursue what they wanted. In place of the fucks they've run out of there now exists an abundance of exciting new ventures and ideas.

The past few years—from the end of the *Love You to Death* era to now in 2022—have shown just how much more the sisters want to grow and evolve their identities, their brand, and the way they operate—all with the freedom of two people who no longer want to cater to anyone but themselves. For *Hey, I'm Just Like You*, Tegan and Sara employed an all-women team, including producer Alex Hope, mixer Beatriz Artola, mastering engineer Emily Lazar, and supporting musicians Carla Azar and Catherine Hiltz. While that wasn't Tegan or Sara's intention going into the studio, everyone involved believed the experience to be really positive; Hope in particular noted that it was a great environment to learn because she felt so supported. Their touring staff has similarly, in recent years, shifted to include more women and people who identify as LGBTQ+.

When you've been in the business for as long as Tegan and Sara, you're able to stand back, look at the bigger picture, and tweak the finer details of your operation. It gives fans, myself included, the hopeful reassurance that Tegan and Sara aren't satisfied being complacent with their success and that they're still trying to identify ways to improve and fully embody that sense of inclusivity that I know they deeply believe in. Those years of enduring prejudices and not fitting in have fuelled them, and now that they're finally feeling empowered by a community that they've worked tirelessly to cultivate and nurture, they're not holding back.

"For me, rather than being scared or worried, now I'm just like, 'Alright, let's go,'" Tegan tells me. "What do we do now, and how do we use everything we just built and continue to add to our empire? We're just getting started."

———————

I have a lot to thank Tegan and Sara for. Their music has gotten me through tough times; their infectious personalities have lifted my spirits when I needed it most. They helped me understand the world from a different perspective, opening my eyes to injustices I was oblivious to for a long time. When I first started researching for this book, I was horrified by the way they'd been written about. I'd been aware of the more egregious attacks on them—the *NME* reviews, the "Wicca-folk" label, the "tampon rock" descriptor—but I couldn't believe those instances were just the tip of the iceberg. In writing my first draft, I was incensed. I called everything out as blatantly homophobic and sexist, boggled by the barbarity of the media, even though I've witnessed much of that malice myself in my years working in music journalism. But it soon hit me that Tegan and Sara, while still carrying some pain from those experiences, have become surprisingly empathetic towards the people who'd treated them like twin lesbian freak shows.

One perspective other writers reminded me of while working on this book is that bad writing isn't inherently malicious, and mainstream monoculture can flatten our ability to be nuanced. So when faced with assessing the genius of Tegan and Sara's music, which lies in its many layers of emotions and meanings, tight deadlines and skinny word counts tended to squeeze out all the nutrients and leave a pile of pulp. This doesn't excuse everything the sisters went through, and questions and jokes around incest, for example, are always unacceptable. But if I've learned anything from my time speaking with Tegan and Sara, it's that kindness and empathy are the most effective and radical ways forward.

While working on this book, my mind was so laser-focused on Tegan and Sara getting critical acclaim because I personally believe that to be a signifier of success, of a legacy triumphantly leaving its mark on music history. But the same monoculture that once worked against artists like Tegan and Sara has burst open in recent years. The definition of success has broadened and having a number-one hit doesn't necessarily mean you're making millions of dollars or packing venues across the country—nor will a negative review tank an entire career. "I think the idea that there's a kind of unilateral critical validation that happens is happening less and less," Sarah Liss told me. Social media has usurped criticism, in many ways. The democratization of voices and opinions on platforms like Twitter, Facebook, YouTube, and more has levelled the playing field, for better and for worse. Now friends, peers, and fans of an artist can congregate online and discuss, dissect, and critique music as soon as it drops, sometimes creating a consensus long before a writer has time to fully form their thoughts in a review published in a more 'traditional' media space. That outdated, perhaps elitist, form of critical validation, it turns out, mattered to me a lot more than it does to most people, including Tegan and Sara. Because to them, knowing that they're effecting change, that they're fostering a bigger and better community of queer artists, and ultimately making their fans happy, are the reasons they're still brimming with ideas today rather than focusing on achieving critical success.

So, fine. Leave Tegan and Sara off your best-of lists. When I spoke with Ronnie Vannucci Jr., he joked that perhaps "only the people that matter" know about them, that some of their power is derived from being a cult favourite. This reminds me of the time I was standing inside a small bar waiting to see British pop artist (and past Tegan and Sara opener) Shura perform. While I was loudly proclaiming that a certain band is one of the most important acts of our lifetime and how frustrated I am that they don't get their due, a woman a few feet away turned over, smiled and asked, "Are you talking about Tegan and Sara?" It was as if she had recognized a secret language I was speaking.

If you've reached the end of this book, I consider you someone now in the know, one of the people Vannucci speaks of: you're one of the people who matter. Tegan and Sara matter.

ENDNOTES

1   Lisa Donato (@DirectorDonato), "I saw Tegan and Sara in 2002 with 10 other people, total. Now they are playing @ the Oscars?! #LGBT #EverythingIsAwesome #Oscars2015," Twitter, February 23, 2015.

2   "Sara Quinn talks about Bruce Springsteen—Hangin' Out," Bruce Springsteen (Official Artist Channel), Youtube, March 3, 2009.

3   Lauren Nostro, "Tegan and Sara's 25 Favourite Albums," *Complex*, January 29, 2013.

4   Kevin Young, "Tegan and Sara," *Canadian Musician Magazine*, January/February 2003.

5   Erin Lyndal Martin, "Shock To Your System: Tegan Of Tegan & Sara Interviewed," *The Quietus*, February 18, 2013.

6   "When Calgary musicians Tegan & Sara were still in high school," *CBC Archives*, March 26, 2021..

7   Kevin O'Keefe, "Music stars Tegan and Sara open up about being twins, their relationship and their sexuality," *CTV* News, February 20, 2020.

8   Ilana Kaplan, "Tegan and Sara: Why There's 'No Excuse' for the Lack of Diversity at Music Festivals," *Glamour*, July 6, 2017.

9   Rachel Lux, "Tegan and Sara: Know Your Role," *Alternative Press*, October 29, 2007.

10 Jenn Pelly and Liz Pelly, "Nine Albums Later, Tegan and Sara Are Finally Ready to Discuss High School," *The New York Times*, September 24, 2019.

11 Associated Press, "Tegan and Sara Reflect on Neil Young's Timeless Advice, Discuss New Musical Direction," *Billboard*, August 8, 2016.

12 Terry Gross. "Tegan and Sara Find Pain—And Unexpected Joy—In 'High School,'" *NPR Music, WPRL*, September 23, 2019.

13 Nina Cocoran, "10 Years with Tegan and Sara: On High School, The L Word, and Growing Up in the 90s," *Consequence*, September 25, 2019.

14 Leslie Ventura, "The Weekly Interview: Sara Quin of Tegan and Sara," *Las Vegas Weekly*, October 19, 2017.

15 Young, "Tegan and Sara."

16 James Keast, "Tegan and Sara: Under Feet Like Ours," *Exclaim*, March 1, 2000.

17 Tegan and Sara (@teganandsara), "Listening to Under Feet Like Ours. I still reject that we (or it) were "folk." The production is way more rock than we were given credit for (then and now). It's still hard to hear parts of it but I think I'm starting to appreciate it (and us). Some of it really is bad ass," Twitter, August 14, 2019.

18 "When Joni Mitchell wore blackface for Halloween," *BBC News*, October 28, 2016.

19 David Koen, "Folk Heroines, Not Heroes," *Phoenix New Times*, August 30, 1989.

20 David Hajdu, "Queer As Folk," *The New York Times*, August 18, 2002.

21 Tom Power, "Fear of coming out stopped Melissa Etheridge from releasing early songs—now, she's ready to be herself," *q with Tom Power*, CBC, October 14, 2021.

22 Zulekha Nathoo, "'You should be heard': Why Tegan and Sara fuse music with activism," *CBC*, June 3, 2018.

23 andythesaint, "Album Review: Tegan and Sara—If It Was You (2002)," *Top Five Reviews, LiveJournal*, February 7, 2005.

24 Patrick Russell, *pomn.com*, January, 2003.

25 dancer_bird, "Song Meanings: Living Room," *SongMeanings*, July 21, 2013.

26 Jane Stevenson, "Tegan and Sara rock out," *Toronto Sun*, 2002.

27 "If It Was You—Tegan and Sara—Vapor Records," *Aversion.com*, August 11, 2002.

28 Will Doig, "Double Down: Tegan and Sara, Sing-Sing," *Metro Weekly*, August 22, 2002.

29 Adrien Begrand, "Tegan and Sara: If It Was You," *popmatters*, August 21, 2002.

30 Mark Redfern, "Letter From the Editor...," *Under the Radar Magazine*, Fall 2005.

31 Rodrigo Perez, "The Next Big Scene: Montreal," *Spin Magazine*, February 2005.

32 David Carr, "Cold Fusion: Montreal's Explosive Music Scene," *The New York Times*, February 6, 2005.

33 "Canada's Most Intriguing Rock Band," *Time Magazine*, April 2005.

34 Tom Beedham, "The Top Charting Canadian Indie Albums of All Time," *INDIE88FM*, February 8, 2017.

35 Jon Dolan, "More New Music to Hear Now," *Spin*, October 2004.

36 Chris Tinkham, "Tegan and Sara on the 10th anniversary of 'So Jealous,'" *Under the Radar*, December 23, 2014.

37 Rodrigo Perez, "Twin Rockers Tegan & Sara Separate So They Can Continue to Work Together," *MTV*, September 29, 2004.

38 Rachel Brodsky, "Q&A: Tegan Quin on 'So Jealous' And Tearing People's Hearts Out," *Spin*, December 22, 2014.

39 Brodsky, "Q&A: Tegan Quin on 'So Jealous' and Tearing People's Hearts Out."

40 Nolan Feeney, "Tegan and Sara: Releasing an Album is Like Running a Political Campaign," *Time*, December 15, 2014.

41 Dr. Stacy L. Smith et al., "Inclusion in the Recording Studio? Gender and Race/Ethnicity of Artists, Songwriters & Producers across 900 Popular Songs from 2012-2020," *USC Annenberg*, March 2021.

42 Tinkham, "Tegan and Sara on the 10th Anniversary of 'So Jealous.'"

43 "You Wouldn't Like Me," "I Won't Be Left," "Where Does the Good Go?," "Downtown," "Fix You Up," "Not Tonight," "Take Me Anywhere."

44 Marc Hogan, "Tegan and Sara: So Jealous," *Pitchfork*, January 14, 2005.

45 Matthew Murphy, "The White Stripes: Walking With a Ghost EP," December 12, 2005.

46 Tim Jonze, "Tegan and Sara: 'We couldn't tell each other we hated being on stage,'" *The Guardian*, June 30, 2016.

47 Eve Barlow, "How 'The Con' Almost Broke Tegan and Sara," *NPR*, October 20, 2017.

48 USC Visions and Voices, "Tegan and Sara in Conversation with Professor Karen Tongson," *Youtube*, April 9, 2021.

49 "Canada Listens 2021: Day 1 Highlights," *CBC Music*, April 12, 2021.

50 Trish Bendix, "Tegan and Sara's Sara Quin on Revisiting 'Profoundly Depressing' Period of Life With 'The Con' Reissue, Tour," *Billboard*, October 12, 2017.

51 Jessica Suarez, "Tegan and Sara: The Con," *Pitchfork*, July 27, 2007.

52 Jessica Hopper, "Lets Further the Discussion," *Tiny Lucky Genius AKA the Unicorn's Tear*, July 27, 2007.

53 Greg Cochrane, "Tegan and Sara: The Con," *NME*, February 15, 2008.

54 Robert Christgau, "The Con," *Rolling Stone*, July 24, 2007.

55 James Rettig, "The Con," *One Week // One Band*, Tumblr, 2015.

56 Peter Knegt, "Tegan and Sara's The Con has given me a decade of catharsis —and here's why that really matters," *CBC Arts*, October 23, 2017.

57 Laura Snapes, "How The Rest of the World Caught Up to Tegan and Sara," *BuzzFeed*, April 7, 2016.

58 Chris Tinkham, "Tegan and Sara: In the Studio," *Under the Radar*, July 16, 2009.

59 Sarah Stead, "Tegan and Sara settle into Sainthood," *The Sheaf*, January 13, 2010.

60 q on cbc, "Tegan & Sara on Q TV," *Youtube*, December 22, 2009.

61 Josiah Hughes, "Exclusive: Tegan and Sara Tap Death Cab For Cutie for Sainthood, Label It "a Very Rocky, Poppy, Heavy Record," *Exclaim*, July 23, 2009.

62 Zharwyn, "07. 'I'm like f*cking Madonna!', Paperback Head—Tegan and Sara, Debaser, Sthlm, Sweden 23/11 2009," *Youtube*, December 19, 2009.

63 Andrzej Lukowski, "Tegan and Sara: Sainthood, Review," *BBC*, 2009.

64 Mammoth Press, "Check out an interview AFI's Hunter Burgan did with Mammoth Press," *Dying Scene*, September 21, 2009.

65 Tegan, "Hell," *Tegan and Sara* (blog), 6 October 2009.

66 Mikael Wood, "Tegan and Sara, 'Sainthood,'" *Spin Magazine*, October 15, 2009.

67 Chris Azzopardi, "Q&A: Indigo Girls Talk 'Fearful' Coming Out, Why Artists Should 'Be Brave' & How Art Will Change Us During Trump," *Pride Source*, January 13, 2017.

68 Tre'vell Anderson, "Cover Star Lil Nas X's Road to Becoming Montero," *Out*, August 3, 2021.

69 Bobby Box, "Why Do Gay Men Idolize Female Pop Stars?," *In Magazine*, October 31, 2019.

70 Snapes, "How The Rest of the World Caught Up to Tegan and Sara."

71 Fuse, "Tegan and Sara On Recording Love You To Death," *Youtube*, December 3, 2006.

72 Michael Tedder, "Grammy-Nominated Adele Producer Greg Kurstin on His Long Road to 'Hello,'" *Billboard*, February 8, 2017.

73 Austin Trunick, "Track-by-Track: Tegan and Sara's Heartthrob Part 1," *Under the Radar*, January 21, 2013.

74 "Song Premiere: Tegan and Sara Grow 'Closer,'" *Rolling Stone*, September 20, 2012.

75 Larissa Pham, "50 Songs That Define the Last 50 Years of LGBTQ+ Pride," *Pitchfork*, June 18, 2018.

76 Marisa Matarazzo, "An Interview With Tegan and Sara," *The Believer*, June 1, 2020.

77 Jason Lipshutz, "Tegan and Sara, 'Heartthrob': Track-By-Track Review," *Billboard*, January 29, 2013.

78 Jon Young, "Tegan and Sara, Heartthrob," *Spin Magazine*, January 29, 2013.

79 Lucy Jones, "Tegan and Sara—'Heartthrob,'" *NME*, February 6, 2013.

80 Joe Reid, "Interview: Darren Stein talks 'G.B.F.' Distribution and a 'Jawbreaker' Musical," *Tribeca News, Tribeca Festival*, October 2, 2013.

81 Warner Records Vault, "Taylor Swift & Tegan and Sara Performing 'Closer' (LIVE AT STAPLES CENTER AUG. 20, 2013)," *Youtube*, August 21, 2013.

82 Billboard, "Tegan & Sara perform 'Just Like a Pill' Live for P!nk at Billboard Women in Music 2013," *Youtube*, January 17, 2014.

83 Nolan Feeney, "Tegan and Sara look back on the 'mayhem' of making The Con: 'I was a disaster,'" *Entertainment Weekly*, October 25, 2017.

84 Elizabeth Goddard [marchingstars], "Tegan and Sara—Support Act intros (Ria Mae + Alex Lahey)," *Youtube*, February 16, 2017.

85 Stéphanie Verge, "The Quin Sisters Want to Change the World," *Lez Spread The Word*, May 30, 2017.

86 Rachel Brodsky, "Review: Tegan and Sara Write the Pop Album They've Earned on Love You to Death," *Spin Magazine*, May 25, 2016.

87 Colin Stutz, "Tegan and Sara Get Stick in a Love Triangle on Poppy New Song 'Boyfriend': Listen," *Billboard*, April 7, 2016.

88 Joe Coscarelli, "Tegan and Sara Talk About 'Love You to Death,' a Deeper Dive Into the Pop Mainstream," *The New York Times*, June 2, 2016.

89 Hattie Collins [Kenzie], "Tegan and Sara on Proud Radio with Hattie Collins," *Youtube*, July 6, 2020.

90 Nolan Feeney, "How Tegan and Sara Became Bona Fide Pop Stars," https://time.com/4286628/tegan-and-sara-interview-love-you-to-death/ (2016, April 20).

91 Spencer Kornhaber, "Tegan and Sara, Scientists of the Love Song," https://www.theatlantic.com/entertainment/archive/2016/06/tegan-and-sara-love-you-to-death-review/485309/ (2016, June 2).

92 Cameron Cook, "Tegan and Sara: Love You to Death," https://pitchfork.com/reviews/albums/21952-love-you-to-death/ (2016, June 8).

93 Jayson Greene, "How Indie Went Pop—and Pop Went Indie—in the 2010s," https://pitchfork.com/features/article/2010s-decade-how-indie-rock-went-pop-bon-iver-grimes-james-blake/ (2019, October 17).

94 Laura Snapes, "How The Rest of the World Caught Up to Tegan and Sara," https://www.buzzfeednews.com/article/laurasnapes/how-the-rest-of-the-world-caught-up-to-tegan-and-sara (2016, April 7).

95 Megan Daley, "Carly Rae Jepsen on new album: 'I was knocking on Tegan and Sara's door myself,'" https://ew.com/article/2015/03/06/carly-rae-jepsen-album-time/ (2015, March 6).

96 Nolan Feeney, "How Tegan and Sara Became Bona Fide Pop Stars," *Time*, April 20, 2016.

97 Brittany Spanos, "Tegan and Sara Launch New Foundation for LGBTQ Girls and Women," *Rolling Stone*, December 19, 2016.

98 Tegan and Sara Foundation, "About the Tegan and Sara Foundation," *Youtube*, June 15, 2017.

99 Leslie Ventura, "The Weekly Interview: Sara Quin of Tegan and Sara," *Las Vegas Weekly*, October 19, 2017.

100 Jules Gor, "Tegan and Sara receive GGPA Award," *CBC News*, *Youtube*, June 2, 2018.

ACKNOWLEDGMENTS

This book would not have been possible without the patience and compassion of my editor, Del Cowie, who helped guide me through the world of publishing. It was his idea to pitch a book about Tegan and Sara, and it was because of his continual encouragement that we are here today with a completed project that I hope we can both feel proud of. He jokes that we may not be friends after this process, but he will never get rid of me. This friendship is forever.

Tegan and Sara's kindness can't be overlooked. I began this process shortly before the COVID-19 pandemic and when I had to cancel my flight to visit the sisters in Vancouver, they agreed to spend numerous hours with me via phone and Zoom instead. Whenever I nervously asked for more time, they graciously obliged when they were likely in the throes of a million other projects. That generosity will never be forgotten.

I would also like to extend a big thank you to Leigh Nash and Norm Nehmetallah, the former and current publishers of Invisible, respectively, both of whom dedicated so much time and effort into making the best possible version of this book. Their expertise gave me full confidence that we could translate my dream and vision into reality.

Joseph Hackett is maybe the only person on Earth who has read every draft of this book, and talked me down from every panic attack I had over the past two years. Somehow, he still wants to stay married to me. I love you, and I hope you're happy this acknowledgement is cemented in print.

Thanks to my CBC Music family for reading and editing my work on a daily basis, and making me a better writer over the past seven years. I'm especially grateful to Holly Gordon and Andrea Warner for reading early drafts of this book and providing constructive edits.

To my friends, thank you for every word of encouragement and for telling me I had to write this book when I first approached you for suggestions of other writers who could be a good fit for this project. You didn't really answer my question, but you gave me all the reassurance I needed to move forward. Special thanks to Jessica Lewis and Aviva Cohen for being my number one supporters and my zine sisters for life.

Lastly, I want to thank every person I spoke to for this book: the musicians, producers, journalists, and, most importantly, Tegan and Sara fans who trusted me with their time, thoughts, and experiences. Without your beautiful insights, this book wouldn't be what it is.

THE BIBLIOPHONIC SERIES is a catalogue of the ongoing history of contemporary music. Each book is a time capsule, capturing artists and their work as we see them, providing a unique look at some of today's most exciting musicians.

INVISIBLE PUBLISHING produces fine Canadian literature for those who enjoy such things. As an independent, not-for-profit publisher, our work includes building communities that sustain and encourage engaging, literary, and current writing.

Invisible Publishing has been in operation for over fifteen years. We released our first fiction titles in the spring of 2007, and our catalogue has come to include works of graphic fiction and nonfiction, pop culture biographies, experimental poetry, and prose.

We are committed to publishing diverse voices and experiences. In acknowledging historical and systemic barriers, and the limits of our existing catalogue, we strongly encourage writers from LGBTQ2SIA+ communities, Indigenous writers, and writers of colour to submit their work.

Invisible Publishing is also home to the Bibliophonic series of music books and the Throwback series of CanLit reissues.

If you'd like to know more, please get in touch:
info@invisiblepublishing.com

Invisible